The Power of Will

The Power of Will:

Key Strategies to Unlock Your Inner Strengths and Enjoy Success in All Aspects of Life

~

Anthony Parinello

~

Chandler House Press
Worcester, Massachusetts
1998

*The Power of Will: Key Strategies to Unlock Your Inner Strengths
and Enjoy Success in All Aspects of Life*

ISBN 1-886284-09-1
Library of Congress Catalog Card Number 97-77505
First Edition
ABCDEFGHIJK

Published by
Chandler House Press
335 Chandler Street
Worcester, MA 01602
USA

President: Lawrence J. Abramoff

Publisher/Editor-in-Chief: Richard J. Staron

Vice President of Sales: Irene S. Bergman

Editorial/Production Manager: Jennifer J. Goguen

Book Design: Bookmakers

Cover Design: Janet Amorello

Chandler House Press books are available at special discounts for bulk purchases. For
more information about how to arrange such purchases, please contact Irene Bergman at
Chandler House Press, 335 Chandler Street, Worcester, MA 01602, or call (800) 642-6657,
or fax (508) 756-9425, or find us on the World Wide Web at www.tatnuck.com.

Chandler House Press books are distributed to the trade by
National Book Network, Inc.
4720 Boston Way
Lanham, MD 20706
(800) 462-6420

Dedication

To my guardian angels:
my mother Josephine Rose
and
my brother Al

∼

*"Be the best **you** that you can be..."*
"I will, I promise."

∼

Contents

Acknowledgments

There are many hands and minds that touch a book before it reaches a bookshelf, many "silent solders" who invest long, hard hours to make sure that the work you hold in your hands is the best that it can be. I thank the individuals at Chandler House who provided corrections, support, and understanding—and the many business associates, friends, family members, and peers who continue to give me the opportunity to be the best me that I can be. I could write a book about all these people! Know as you read this book that it has been brought to you not only by me, but also by an army of people who have, in various ways, shown a light on the pathway of an extraordinary life.

Specific recognition goes out to... Catherine Jones, our "tower of power," for true grit and determination... Diane Durbin, for keeping Parinello Incorporated running... my sister Phyllis Ann Cassia, for proofreading and suggestions... Brandon Toropov, for ideas, words, and creativity... Dick Staron, for giving me the great gift of opportunity... Jennifer Goguen, for her thoughtful design and production help... Dennis Latham, for tireless editing work... Susan Glinert, for her top-notch graphics and artwork... Irene Bergman, for superior sales and marketing efforts... and Janet Amorello for wrapping it all up with a beautiful cover design.

A special thanks to you!

None of this would be possible without you, my new friend. Without your unique needs, interests, and dreams, there might as well be no book at all!

Introduction

Growing up in a tough town like Hoboken, New Jersey, is quite an experience. I know because I did it! Back in the fifties, walking home from school could quickly turn into a hands-on lesson in self-defense. One boy we called "Spike" always seemed ready to leap out at me from behind a stoop as I returned home in the afternoon! As a kid in Hoboken, I developed a keen awareness that came with inner-city life, an awareness that prepared me for unexpected challenges waiting just around the corner. The challenges in my life have changed since then, but they've never vanished entirely. I bet this is true in your life, too. Something always waits over the next hill or around the corner. I think the question isn't so much "What could it be?" as "How will we respond to it?" In this book, we will look at many challenges and find the best ways to use your internal powers to meet them in a way that points you toward a happier, more fulfilling life.

People often ask me: How did you become a motivational speaker and author? Well, it certainly wasn't from my youthful interest in literature or drama—I didn't have any—and it wasn't because I had an innate gift for motivating others that early in my life. I found my real passion at age 40, after a successful career as a salesperson. Since moving into my next career, I've helped over one million professionals from all walks of life to accelerate the process of finding the "true self"—the self that harnesses what I call the Power of Will. This is a process that took me four decades to complete. I believe, that if you take full advantage of this book, you won't have to wait that long.

During one of our notorious pool games, I told my father that I was writing a new book called *The Power of Will.* He immediately asked me, "What's Will's last name?" We both chuckled. I didn't have the answer, but I did use dad's question to look at this endeavor from another angle. After pondering Will's identity for a while, I came to some conclusions.

Will is the person you admired most while you were growing up. The bright, levelheaded person in your class that you always hoped would be your best friend. The main character in the novel that made the biggest positive impact on you. He or she is the person who has moved past fear, who learned how to make the right things happen. The person who always figured it all out, the person who grabbed the gold ring on the merry-go-round.

In other words, Will (or Wilhelmina) is the person *we want to be when we grow up.* In this book, you'll learn to acquire the resources to help you become your own Will—to help you build and live out your dream while you're awake, inspired, and here on planet earth. I know you'll find, by the end of our time together, that *being* Will is a lot more exciting than simply *wishing* you were Will. Making that kind of change in your life is going to take some hard work, and you must be ready to learn more about yourself than you've ever learned in the past. You must be willing to remove—or, at the very least, minimize—any and all self-imposed barriers that have kept you from fulfilling your true purpose in life.

You'll notice that, on the first page of each chapter of this book, there is a graphic representation of a wall. I've selected this image because, to me, a wall is something that separates, isolates, and defines an area that someone (or something) has determined we should not experience or understand. Over the past half-century, I've broken down many of the walls that have held me back and kept me from growing, kept me from experiencing all that life has to offer. I know you can do the same to the walls in your life. Don't get me wrong: Growth is an ongoing process, and I still have my share of "renovation" to carry out! (In fact, I sometimes feel as though I should post a sign outside my office that reads, "Pardon the dust during *my* renovation!)

As you make your way through the book, you'll also notice that the wall gets smaller and smaller with each new chapter—until finally, it disappears entirely in Chapter Ten. This is not an optical illusion or an error in the book's layout—it's a metaphor. The key is to recognize where the walls are in our lives, and to make the choices that will help us dismantle them. Every chapter in *The Power of Will* includes ideas, concepts, and insights that will help you demolish disabling walls and barriers.

Sure—bringing down a wall is a big job. Don't worry if you haven't been able to do it in the past. This time, you've got a coach. Together, you and I can accomplish much more than we would if we were to go it alone. I invite you to...

Follow me closely, but cast your own shadow.

And then, once you've made your dream a reality, once you've become your own Will, once you've made it to the top of your own mountain, I hope you'll help someone else get to the top of his or her peak. That's why I created this book, and I hope it will be your purpose as you put it to use.

Let's turn the page... together!

~ Chapter 1 ~

The Mountain

Think of a time in your life when you accomplished something that, at one time, had seemed impossible.

Perhaps everyone had told you that you had no chance to get the job you were after, win a date with a special person, or attain an important personal, financial, spiritual, or business goal. All the odds seemed stacked against you, and yet somehow you became "single minded." You set your sights on the goal that energized you, summoned your resources, focused yourself, and attained the "impossible."

Virtually everyone has had at least one experience like this (although many people seem to go out of their way to avoid remembering these events). What force was at work when you initiated these powerful changes? And how can you put that force to work on a regular basis? We'll examine those questions in this first chapter. You'll start by finding out what the Power of Will is (and isn't). You'll learn about the role your opinions, beliefs, and convictions have played in getting you this far in life—and what affect these forces can have on your destiny. You will learn more about your outlook on the subject of committing to positive change, and you'll get important insights on how to avoid being distracted by the challenges and issues that may stand between you and the ability to put the Power of Will to work in every aspect of your life.

Willpower

Take a moment, right now, and recall a specific time when you told yourself, "This is it"— and followed through on a daunting goal.

Perhaps you decided to quit smoking, stop overeating, get more exercise, or escape a dead-end job or relationship. Perhaps you came to the conclusion that it was time to become more disciplined about finishing your education, spending more time with your family and friends, worshipping on a more regular basis, or donating more time or money to a worthwhile cause. Whatever your "this is it" decision was, you accepted, on some level, that change requires a serious, focused effort—a state of mind that many people miscategorize, I believe, as "willpower."

In my book (which, fortunately enough, you happen to be reading at the moment!), willpower is not the same as the Power of Will. Let's look at the differences.

To me, the popular word "willpower" suggests struggle—a possible ongoing conflict between certain objectives and opposing temptations or distractions. When I use the words the Power of Will in this book, however, I'm referring to something very different—a deep, even profound certainty about who we are, what we're doing, and what our deepest purposes are.

These are two very different ideas! Consider this example. As he steps out from the shower and beholds his once-trim physique in the full-length mirror, a voice inside Brandon's head is saying: "I really need to slim down. I don't like the way my clothes fit these days. I need to drop 15 pounds before the holidays get here or I'm going to be in trouble, big time, when they start passing around the turkey and trimmings!" So Brandon wants to lose weight. But here's the question—is he certain about that goal yet?

It doesn't take long to find out. That night, he finishes the dinner dishes and hears something strange. He notices that the vanilla ice cream seems to be calling his name seductively from the freezer! "Brandon..." it whimpers, "I'm lonely. Come play with me..."

"Oh, well," he tells himself on the way to the kitchen, "one scoop can't hurt." Before you know it, one scoop becomes several scoops, and soon Brandon tells himself, "Well, I'm almost done, and I sure don't want to waste freezer space. I might as well knock off this last little bit. After this half gallon is gone, I simply won't buy another for at least a month!" (Rationalization is a wonderful thing, isn't it?) As he prepares to demolish the last of the ice cream, he hears a low but persistent voice that makes him stop short—for a moment. "What are you *doing*?" it asks. "You've overdone it again. Don't you know Aunt Carol is going to be here for Thanksgiving, and looking for any opportunity to make a snide remark about your midsection? Put that spoon down immediately! You have to lose some weight, and you're going to start... right now!"

Well, Brandon wants to diet. But not right away. He decides to ignore the "drop-the-spoon" voice and pay attention to the "conserve freezer space" voice. Later, feeling guilty, he tells himself that he should have had enough willpower to skip the ice cream.

The reality is that the louder, stronger, more convincing, more persistent, and more dominant voice in these struggles will always win. This time around, the seductive call of ice cream outweighed the possibility of a few more barbed remarks from Aunt Carol. Brandon was involved in a mental tug of war *with himself.* The habit he tried to break, and the change he tried to make, became suspended between yes and no, doing it or not, making it happen or letting it happen.

This (often-relentless) internal conflict saps energy, and sometimes takes an enormous toll. And often, even after achieving success—even after you've lost weight and deprived Aunt Carol of conversational material—there is a possibility that the "victory" may be short-lived. We're constantly tempted, and temptation can become too much to resist. Our willpower often slips. Someone offers to take us out for ice cream, or suggests we splurge and buy that new sports coat, even though the credit card is nearly maxed out! In a flash, all the old habits are instantly reestablished. Sometimes, no matter how much we "win," we eventually lose!

Willpower, as it's commonly understood, is susceptible to forces beyond control. These include: external situations such as social pressure and temptation, stress, unrewarding interpersonal relationships, financial problems, challenges at the office, and so on. These situations can (and often do) make our temptation voice louder than our compliance voice. In the end, one part of us wins and the other part loses.

The Power of Will

When I use the phrase the Power of Will, I'm talking about a force quite separate from willpower as it's generally defined. When the Power of Will works, there is *one and only one* voice inside your head—the right voice. When you have the Power of Will up and running, you simply act as you believe. Your decision to act, or not act, matches your innermost thoughts, values, and voices.

There is no "tug of war," no lost energy, and no conflict. Your energies are focused toward a single goal: your chosen goal. The power of will says that you are one, that your actions take the same direction as your desires, and your desires match your values. The result: congruency, happiness, and total fulfillment in every area of your life in which you feel this kind of certainty. You don't struggle over whether or not (for instance) to eat red meat; you act on a carefully considered, strongly motivated personal decision that's based upon certain values, qualities, traits, beliefs, and convictions. You eliminate red meat from your life. You vow never to look back! You make a promise to yourself— and you respect that promise enough to keep it.

Putting the Power of Will to Work

People who put the Power of Will to work in their lives have purpose and resolve. They don't simply "desire" or "wish for" outcomes—they're on a well-defined mission! They are self-determined people, a little like Yoda in *The Empire Strikes Back*. You may remember the advice he gave Luke Skywalker when Luke said he'd "try" to do something: "No—there is no try. Do. Or do not."

To learn how to put your own Power of Will to work, you'll need to get in touch with what gives you that power in the first place: You! You are your best ally or worst enemy when it comes to harnessing the force under discussion: a formidable sense of purpose that arises from your own opinions, beliefs and convictions.

Let's look at each of these three (very different) categories now.

❀ *Opinions* fall short of positive knowledge. An opinion is a combination of facts and ideas that are probably true or likely to be proven true. It is possible to have one or more opinions on the same topic. It is also easy and acceptable in business and social circumstances to change an opinion. It's also possible to have no opinion on a certain subject!

❀ *Beliefs* are based upon past experiences, generalizations, or conjecture. Once a belief is obtained, it's generally held to be true and is rarely challenged or changed. Sometimes, we are tempted to defend our beliefs to the bitter end— even when there may be no factual basis for the belief!

❀ *Convictions* are certainties of the mind in either of the previous two categories—that is, fully settled opinions or assured beliefs. Once established, convictions defy alteration. In extreme situations, convictions can cause serious financial, social, and physical setbacks. Convictions can also be responsible for total success in every aspect of life.

Of all three factors, beliefs hold the greatest influence over who we are and how we envision our purpose on earth. Our beliefs affect the quality of our lives, futures, reason, overall state of being, and level of happiness or sadness. Beliefs are the core of how we form opinions and develop convictions. They form the basis for how we look at the world and everything in it.

Our beliefs affect our actions and how we feel physically at any given moment. Countless experiments and tests have proven that once your mind forms a belief, your body will react to and follow that belief, even if that reaction is not proper, common, predicted—or logical!

~

Your mind does not know the difference between a real experience and a perceived experience. When it encounters a belief that is firm enough, it treats that belief as though it were reality, and so it becomes reality.

~

Virtually every noteworthy university has studied the topic of beliefs and their effect on mind/body relationships. In one study, 100 participants were divided into two groups of 50. Each group took a different drug: one a moderately potent tranquilizer, and the other an equally potent stimulant. What the participants didn't know was that they weren't getting what they thought they were!

Fifty participants who thought they were going to get the tranquilizer got the stimulant instead, and fifty who thought they were getting the stimulant received the tranquilizer. In *every* case, the "reaction" to the drug was exactly opposite to what was in the pill, but precisely in line with the "expectation" caused by the belief.

Imagine that! If the human mind can overpower a potent drug, what could it do if it worked in concert with consciously chosen beliefs?

Beware!

In many cases, the question isn't *whether* we're going to develop strong beliefs and a sense of purpose—but rather what we will allow our minds to become highly purposeful *about*. If we don't take control by understanding, challenging, and changing our beliefs according to a conscious plan, then someone or something else will! In the end, I believe that's what putting the Power of Will to work is all about: taking full responsibility for constructing beliefs that empower you as a person to live a more fulfilling and rewarding life, beliefs that leave you feeling as certain as Yoda about what you're doing (or not doing). The alternative? Being manipulated by others!

You may think I'm getting too worked up about the potentially devastating effects of failing to harness your own Power of Will and allowing others to manage your beliefs. I'm not paranoid— but I'm not kidding, either. Researchers have spent millions of dollars to confirm the fundamental truth I am talking about. Anyone—repeat, anyone—can control key aspects of life and the future by taking control of certain parts of the mind. Clearly, the advertising industry has taken full advantage of this research, but they're not alone! We are all in danger of having our brains "co-opted" by various accomplished belief-shifters, both professional and amateur: superiors, manipulative family members, and unscrupulous politicians, to name only a few. To take full advantage of the Power of Will, you must resolve to take control of your *own* mind. This book will show you how to do that in all the important areas.

Credibility and Social Proof

How are beliefs manipulated? In that dramatic study involving tranquilizers and sedatives, the credibility of the doctors conducting the test, and the official-feeling test environment itself, had powerful affects on the outcome. So did the actions of other people.

A belief in certain patterns was "installed" through information from a credible source—namely, doctors who told participants exactly what was going to happen. As a result, one or two participants began to have the predicted reaction; then something called "social proof" came into play. As other participants witnessed the changes, they found it easier and more acceptable to make that predicted reaction their own.

We've all been witnesses to the power of social proof. Haven't you ever behaved a little differently in a crowd than you would have if you'd been sitting alone in a room? Sometimes it doesn't take much more than being a witness to the behavior of other people for a belief to be installed in our brains. Once it's there, our bodies react powerfully, and often automatically.

Several years ago, a group of air travelers were in flight from Los Angeles to Narita, Japan. About four hours from their destination, several passengers became violently ill. Before this ordeal was over, more than 100 passengers also became ill, and at least 50 were taken from the Narita airport by ambulance once the plane landed.

This was major news in Japan. The illness was traced to food poisoning. Yet, amazingly, many passengers who *had not* eaten any spoiled food became temporarily ill! (You may be wondering how I know the details about what was eaten by the unfortunate flight "victims." The answer: My wife was the head flight attendant!)

The food-poisoning story illustrates how our beliefs—in this case, beliefs installed by social influences—play an important role in determining our actions and reactions at a deep level. A similar principle worked in the famous study that demonstrated that under-performing students were likely to perform better on standardized tests when their *teachers* were informed (inaccurately) that previous tests had identified the children as highly gifted. In other words, when a teacher genuinely believed a new student to be a prodigy, the student often performed well— even if he or she had struggled in the past!

~

*Given the right stimulation and environment, a suffi-
ciently powerful belief will put our minds through whatever experience is necessary to validate the belief.*

~

Time out—something really terrible just happened to me. As
I was sitting at my computer writing this book, and eating a
hard pretzel, one of my fillings fell out! I hate it when that happens! It's like putting aluminum foil in your mouth and chew-
ing. As I type these words, the sensation makes chills run down
my spine. Now my tongue feels like it's found the world's larg-
est crater right there on the lower right-hand side of my mouth.
I know what has to happen now, and I'm not looking forward to
it (which is probably why I'm writing all this instead of picking
up the phone and calling my dentist). I dread the feeling of the
dentist putting all those awful-tasting metallic instruments in
my mouth. Then there's that awful whirring noise and the smell of
his drilling. I hate smelling my teeth as they're burning and grind-
ing away under the mosquito-times-fifty whine of that drill!

Now, at some level, did you just relive your last visit to the
dentist? Did your mouth pucker up, jaw start to tighten and
your teeth start to feel funny? If so, you've experienced a simple
instance of the power suggestion can have on your mind—and the
power your mind can have over your body's sensory mechanism!

Every Belief Has Its Supporting Elements

What makes us so "gullible"? Is the power of suggestion really
that powerful? In a word, yes. Our brain is complex, but in many
settings, it acts on very basic principles. It relies upon certain
basic stimuli to prompt a reaction.

Consider the case of the Narita flight passengers. Some felt ill
for a good reason: they actually ate the spoiled food. As these
passengers displayed symptoms of stomach cramps, nausea,
and vomiting, there was a commotion. People pushed call buttons,
flight attendants rushed up and down the aisles, and the captain

announced that the "situation" was under control and passengers should not be concerned. Yet, when a healthy passenger asked a flight attendant what the ill passengers had eaten, her reply ("the beef") triggered the next wave of "ill" passengers!

Eventually, the flight crew determined the problem was *not* bad beef, but that didn't stop the social influences—spurred by the initial input from a credible source—from wreaking havoc. Many who had eaten the beef began to display the same conditions as the passengers who had actually eaten spoiled food: stomach cramps, nausea, and vomiting. As I mentioned earlier, our brains simply do not know the difference between real and imaginary conditions!

Reading a story like this makes me wonder—and I hope it makes you wonder—what might happen if we proactively and selectively seek and harness information and knowledge from credible sources and social proof, instead of letting ourselves react to these same influences!

Control Your Own Beliefs!

It's virtually impossible to understate the importance of beliefs when it comes to harnessing the Power of Will. Beliefs are not always easy to change, but it's worth the effort to learn how to change them. It's a matter of applying the right stimuli. With a little practice applying those stimuli, you can quickly change or install such beliefs as:

- § I feel sick.
- § I feel stupid.
- § I feel depressed.
- § I'm a great student.
- § I am the luckiest person in the world!
- § My determination makes me unstoppable!

To get started, let's focus on the three conditions necessary for our mind to change, strengthen, or install beliefs.

☘ Understanding and accepting information from a credible source (A flight attendant or pilot's authoritative voice making an important intercom announcement, or a doctor's powerful statement or diagnosis).

☘ Witnessing emotional situations and responding to social proof of the belief (The physical response or discomfort of others or a teacher's decision to read the best papers in class aloud).

☘ Gathering or creating new information or strengthening original information ("The beef is bad" or "I have a great memory for facts and figures").

Let's look at each of these conditions in more detail.

Information from Credible Sources

When we hear a message from persons of authority—people we respect—we tend to believe that message to be the truth, or at least consider the possibility that what the person is saying is true.

There are certain people and organizations we respect and view as credible. If Siskel and Ebert give a film "two thumbs up," millions of people are likely to attend that film *with the expectation that they will enjoy the film*—which certainly doesn't hurt the odds that they actually *will* enjoy it. The same principle applies to messages we receive from celebrities, members of the clergy, respected news analysts, and all kinds of other "credible sources." Whether or not a given source *should* be credible is a separate question. Each of us has identified people and institutions we respect. Such figures can lack universal credibility, but the credible-source principle is pretty reliable. Few of us would instinctively "tune out" a trusted doctor's advice if we were violently ill for a reason we didn't understand.

Emotional Situations and Social Proof

When others act in an emotionally charged way, the action can be contagious. The more intense the emotion, the more likely we are to take on and display similar emotions—even if we try not to do so! Perhaps something like this has happened to you in a movie theater during a four-hanky blockbuster. Even if you're not usually one to cry, if others around you are getting choked up about the situation being portrayed on-screen, you'll be more likely to respond emotionally. Have you ever noticed what happens at the end of a rousing speech in a crowded auditorium? If people up front rise for a standing ovation, chances are the rest of the audience will, too. Other people influence our emotions and our reactions.

In addition to the influences of other people, our own sensory experiences affect our belief structures in a similar way. Whether we're experiencing sadness, happiness, pain, or pleasure, the more senses of sight, smell, taste, sound, and feelings we use, the greater the emotional experience. And the greater the emotional experience, the stronger the belief. That's why good motivational speakers play music, encourage physical actions, and use visual displays to inspire their audiences. These emotional "boosters" are fundamental catalysts of change!

Gathering or Creating Original Information

Your facts and information can come from any source—or no source at all. Again: Your mind doesn't know the difference between real or imagined events! This definitely includes information. If you can gather or create data that will support an existing belief, it will automatically become stronger. The more supportive information you add, the stronger your belief will become—until it eventually develops into a conviction. Because convictions tend to stick around forever, the ones we embrace have a huge impact on the quality of our lives. Latching on to the *right* convictions can mean prosperity, optimism, and happiness. Latching on to the wrong convictions can literally kill you.

Shape Your Future!

What have we established so far? A belief is a thought in our mind that we hold to be true. We rarely question or challenge where a given belief comes from, and to some extent we will protect that belief without question.

~

Having a belief simply means that your mind is certain on a given topic. The trick is to become certain about the right things—and to avoid perpetuating conflicting beliefs that cause internal struggles and block personal growth.

~

Beliefs play a huge role in determining whether we are open or closed to new ideas, experiences, opportunities, and relationships. Many beliefs are not consciously chosen and not healthy! To take advantage of the Power of Will, we need to examine and question our beliefs—and replace our disabling beliefs with enabling ones. Ultimately, we'll want to transform our most powerful, constructive beliefs into convictions.

Disabling and Enabling Beliefs

- I've never been any good with people.
- I've been out of work for four months—if I haven't found the right job by now, I probably never will.
- My parents ruined me for life.
- I'm too short to make the basketball team.
- My arms are too weak for me to take up golf.

These are examples of what I call "killer beliefs." They sabotage future growth and kill part of your potential for future growth—unless you uninstall them! Many of these beliefs are the result of someone else's prejudice, a single bad experience, or the cumulative effects of our own social, economic and physical environment. A fair number of disabling beliefs are cultivated by people hoping to take advantage of us—and, too often, they succeed in doing so.

Here's the good news: it takes a lot less energy to hold enabling beliefs than to hold disabling ones! To uninstall killer beliefs, we must stop treating our past—or what we've been taught to believe about our past—as the key determinant of our future. We must stop replaying things that may or may not have taken place in the past—and begin looking toward the purpose that can guide us as we build the future!

To take full advantage of the Power of Will, *you must be willing to get rid of the killer beliefs that have held you down in the past and look ahead in your life!* This will not always be easy, but it's always in your best interest to make the effort.

When you're tempted to fixate on a past problem and reinforce a killer belief, ask yourself:

~

Why do they make the windshield of a car so much bigger than the rear view mirror?

~

Building the Bridge to Your Future: Your Most Powerful Beliefs

The world-famous George Washington Bridge—or GWB, as it is called by the locals—spans the Hudson River. Connecting New Jersey with New York, it carries tens of thousands of commuters each day. This bridge was built in 1931 using the still popular suspension bridge technology. Suspension bridges have two vertical pillars connected by two independent cables attached to anchors on all four points. Each of these elements depends upon the other for the strength to suspend the roadway.

What does this have to do with confirming or changing your existing beliefs and your future? Everything! Like our enabling beliefs, the great bridge is a connector. You need strong enabling beliefs to get you from where you are today to where you want to be in your future.

One side of the "belief bridge" is attached to your present; the other rests on the shore of your future. Every supporting element, every enabling belief, supports the road to your future. Remember, the more information you possess from a credible source, the more you witness emotional situations and gain social proof and relevant new or original information, the stronger your beliefs will become. Which beliefs will you reinforce? What are your enabling core beliefs?

An enabling core belief is one that serves as the bridge that will lead you where you want to go. Here is one of my core beliefs:

§   I am a special, compassionate person, here on this earth to help others.

My mother planted this belief in my mind many years ago. Who knows where she got that belief, or why she chose to plant it in *my* mind? I only know that she repeated it time and time again as I was growing up—until I had accepted it at a very deep level.

This was by no means the only enabling belief my mother passed along! She also encouraged initiative in my life. She constantly reinforced the belief that I would benefit from taking action on my own behalf. Her messages in support of this idea were many and varied:

§   Ask for the opportunity, raise, or promotion.

§   Let others know what you're doing, and how good you are or can be.

§   Be modest but, when the time is right, don't hesitate to step forward.

§   Do what you can do; then, at the right time, let people know that you've done it.

Growing up in an inner city wasn't easy, but with my mother's constant encouragement, I made it through all right. I suspect I wouldn't be doing what I'm doing now, helping others through my seminars, videos, audios, and this book, if my mom hadn't constantly put positive, uplifting beliefs into my mind. She knew I had to build strong bridges.

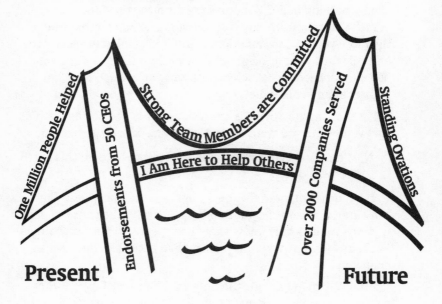

Above is an illustration of a "belief bridge." You will note that my core belief is supported by two major elements, which are the bridge uprights. They give my core belief—about being a special person, and being here to help others—credibility. The following are two facts that come from credible sources that support my enabling belief (*Understanding and accepting information from a credible source*):

$ Over fifty CEOs have personally praised me for my unique ideas.

$ Over 2,000 companies have paid to take advantage of my exceptional speaking skills.

Notice a strong supporting cable—in this case, "social proof"— supports my belief. Here, we're not just talking about "endorsements," but about connections that have a significant amount of emotion attached to them. (*Witnessing emotional situations, social proof, and gathering or creating new information or strengthening original information.*) Take a look:

- ❧ I have positively affected the lives of over one million people.
- ❧ I have strong team members who are committed to my vision.
- ❧ I have received countless standing ovations.

As you can see, I have incorporated all three ingredients to reinforce the core belief that I am a special, compassionate person, here to help others. (As you may have already noticed, the last two elements can dovetail.)

- ❀ Facts from a credible source
- ❀ Emotional situations and social proof
- ❀ Gathering or creating new information or strengthening original information

This, then, is an enabling belief—one I constantly reinforce and use to point myself toward my future.

You Try It!

Now, it's time to create your own bridge and develop or strengthen a powerful, enabling belief. To start, think about a belief that you already exercise without too much difficulty—one you share regularly with everyone around you and one that you are known for. For instance, you may already agree strongly with one or more the following statements.

- ❧ I believe that every day is a great day!
- ❧ I believe that we should live for the present moment, because that's just what it is—a present!
- ❧ I believe I can always bounce back after a setback.

§ I believe that I can do anything that I set my mind to.

§ I believe that my love for my family will enrich all of my future endeavors.

Now, using my bridge concept, draw or trace a suspension bridge on a large piece of paper, and then follow the instructions below:

❀ **Step 1**: Write an enabling belief across the suspension or roadway. IMPORTANT! Whenever you write an enabling belief you must write it in the first person and write it positively! For example:

Whenever a door slams shut, I know greater opportunity is behind it!

❀ **Step 2**: Pick two facts from a credible source that support your enabling belief. Write these on the two uprights. If you have more than two major supporting facts, pick the two strongest. In our example, that might be:

My mother and father survived the Great Depression. They prospered and helped me understand the real source of our family's material and emotional wealth: each other.

My family includes many entrepreneurs who have made a daily habit of "turning lemons into lemonade."

❀ **Step 3**: Write three supporting social proof statements on one of the cables. Remember, social proof statements should always have emotion attached to them. For example:

My boss has told me many times that I'm highly creative.

People come to me for help when they are really stuck on difficult problems—and they feel better after I've helped them.

I received the "Employee of the Month" award twice for solving difficult problems.

✵ **Step 4**: Now, write down three facts that you've gathered and place one on each of the three portions of the cable. Remember, in this step it's best to use your strongest facts to illustrate each of the three conditions necessary for your brain to change, strengthen or install a belief. You can use "hard data" or develop your own positive assumptions about yourself, but in either case what you write down must support your enabling belief. For example:

I am persistent.

I can do anything I set my mind to.

I've already accomplished things that other people considered difficult or impossible.

Future Exercises

I suggest that you identify at least five enabling core beliefs, and then create a "bridge" for every single one of them.

Back in 1931, the GWB was built on such a solid foundation and such sound technology that they were able to add another roadway to it 55 years after it was built! If your enabling core beliefs are strong and based upon solid reasoning, you'll be able to add to your own bridge as time goes by.

Convictions

Convictions are the most powerful form of beliefs. Convictions add purpose, resolve, focus, and acceleration to your beliefs.

Think of a time when you were totally convinced of something—and this conviction led you to support a political cause, or do volunteer or outreach work, or become a member of a committee, or whatever (as long as it wasn't criminal!). You wanted the world to know it and to feel the same or even greater devotion to your cause. You even prepared rebuttals for anyone who opposed your conviction!

Here is a very simple illustration of the difference between beliefs and convictions. Suppose you had the following belief:

 ֍ All pets should be spayed and neutered.

You would be sympathetic to that cause and hold it in a special place in your heart. You would encourage others to take care of their pets, and if somebody approached you at the local supermarket with a petition to make it mandatory to spay and neuter all household animals, you would certainly sign it and thank the person for their efforts.

But if you had a *conviction* about the importance of all pets being spayed and neutered, you would probably be the one at the supermarket holding the clipboards and requesting signatures. You would donate time and money to the cause, put bumper stickers on your car, give talks at various organizations, and perhaps start a clinic and offer to neuter pets for next to nothing! If you did all this, you would have a true conviction that all pets should be spayed and neutered. See the difference?

Where do convictions come from? They build over time. If we're not careful, *disabling* opinions and beliefs can also become convictions. So we have to be careful about the beliefs we reinforce, and we have to identify and root out beliefs that hold us back. One good way to do this is to ask questions like:

 ֍ Where did I get this belief?

 ֍ How long ago did I adopt this belief?

 ֍ Have I ever compromised this belief? If so, how many times? How long ago? Why?

 ֍ What have been the consequences, if any, when this belief was compromised?

 ֍ What would happen to my health, finances, and personal and professional life if I eliminated this belief?

Once you've used this process to identify a disabling belief ("I'm too young to make a positive impact at work"), you should install a corresponding positive belief. (For instance: "My youth gives me fresh perspectives and a high energy level that no one else at work offers.") So use the bridge exercise—fast!—when you identify a negative, disabling belief. Set up a corresponding positive, enabling belief—so that the positive belief can turn into a conviction!

As you move forward, chapter by chapter, in *The Power of Will*, you'll find more advice on uprooting disabling beliefs and installing constructive, enabling beliefs that support your future growth. But the basics you've learned about in this chapter serve as the foundation for what follows.

Have you taken the time to complete the bridge exercise for at least five positive core beliefs? Did you put the exercise off because you were "too busy"—or because you wanted to wait until your surroundings "settled down" a little bit or you wanted to finish this chapter first? If so, remember:

~

Kites take off and fly when they are put up against the wind.

Every single journey has just one starting point.

If you want to build something big you must first start with something small.

You aren't reading this book because you want your life to remain the way it is.

~

Sure, it would be easier to watch your sitcom tonight than to complete this exercise. If change came easy, everyone would do it! To get the most out of this book, you'll need to develop your "determination" muscle. Let the bridge exercise be your first opportunity to "work out" in this all-important area.

Don't do the exercise because I'm telling you to—do the exercise because you want to build a better, more fulfilling, more purposeful, more self-determined future for yourself—a future in which you take full advantage of the Power of Will.

Self-determination

How important is it to be self-determined? Well, it's not important at all if you want to let someone else control your future.

In the following chapters, you will be asked to work hard. You will be asked to find out what got you this far in your life. To get to the next level, you'll have to question everything! You'll have to learn to discard what is disabling and enhance what is enabling—not laboriously, but almost by reflex!

Let me tell you a little story about why this discarding and enhancing process is so important. When I turned 50 years old in 1997, I thought I should do something epic to celebrate. I decided to run the Pike's Peak Marathon. I've run a few marathons, but the Pike's Peak run is considered more than just a "casual" marathon. It happens to be the toughest marathon in North America because it *starts* at 6,500 feet above sea level. You run up a trail to 14,110 feet, the summit of Pike's Peak. This is the halfway point! Then you run back down the mountain, to finish almost where you started, at 6,800 feet above sea level.

I started training for this race months ahead of time. I ran, ate all the right stuff, ran, bought the right equipment, ran, ate, ran... ran, ate, ran, bought, ran, ate, ran, bought... Well, you get the picture. I ate about 17 pounds of pasta (that's called carbo-loading), ran about 520 miles and bought about $1,200 in Power Bars, chemicals, running shoes and shorts. Self-determined, filled with purpose, resolve, intention, and pasta, I headed to Colorado four days early. That schedule, I decided, would give me plenty of time to acclimate myself to the altitude.

Driving down the highway toward Colorado Springs, I saw a mountain. I pulled off the road to get my map out, and sure enough—it was Pike's Peak, all 14,110 feet of it. You can't miss this most prominent geographical feature. At first, I felt a bit intimidated—but I'd done all the right things as far as food, training, gear, and so forth. I wasn't going to turn back! I drove on.

A few hours later, I was checking into my hotel. To my left, at the front desk, a large picture window gave a terrific view of

Pike's Peak. It was a beautiful day. I mentioned to the young man checking me in, "That's a great view of Pike's Peak you've got!"

"Yeah," he replied, "It sure is." He paused for a moment, then said: "You're not running that marathon, are you?" I told him I was. His instant response took me by surprise: "Man, you're crazy. People die up there!"

For a second, self-doubt hit me. What if I wasn't ready? What if I did get in trouble? Maybe I hadn't done enough training!

That night, I went out to dinner. I had to carbo-load! I needed lots of pasta. Sitting next to me was a person who appeared to be a runner (his second plate of pasta was a dead giveaway). I struck up a conversation with him and learned that he, too, was running Pike's Peak. Ah! A peer! An opportunity for a little camaraderie! We started talking about running. My new friend told me he had run five ultra-marathons. An ultra-marathon is a *100-mile* race, making the standard 26-mile run seem like a jog around the block. This guy had run five of them! I didn't have his experience! What was I doing getting ready to run up Pike's Peak?

The next night, I went out to dinner, carbo-loading once again. (You can't really get enough carbohydrates before a long distance run.) This time I struck up a conversation with a woman sitting next to me. She was about 50 years old and she, too, was running Pike's Peak. I started to feel a bit more comfortable— until I found out that she was in the middle of running one marathon a week for 50 consecutive weeks. One marathon in each of the 50 states. All the self-determination in the world couldn't help me get a good night's sleep that night. I tossed and turned and wondered, "What on earth have I gotten into?"

The morning of the race arrived. I got my shoes, my backpack, 10 Power Bars, chemical additives for my drinking water, and my Gortex jacket. I was as ready as I could be. At the start of the race, I tried to forget that I was probably outclassed, and tried to focus on all my training and preparation. Thank God it was cloudy. If I could have seen the mountain peak, I probably would have quit before I started! I remember thinking that I hadn't had time to come to terms with the possible impact of what I had gotten into, when—bang! The starting gun went off and I was running up the trail, moving toward the summit of Pike's Peak.

Back and forth, higher and higher, back and forth again, right through the clouds. At 12,500 feet, there are no trees. The steep trail gets narrow and rocky. The air gets so thin at that altitude that it's hard to breathe as you run.

Well, I'll make a long story short for you—I completed the course. But you know what? Even with all the training, eating all the right food, drinking and staying focused, I still had to stop six times during that race. Six times I was virtually paralyzed. Even with all of my self-determination, purpose, resolve—my friends Howard and Jane Price and my family waiting at the finish line—even then I simply couldn't take another step.

Can you guess what stopped me dead in my tracks six times? Cramps? No, stretching and drinking and eating the right replacement chemicals saved me from that problem. Doubt? Well, there does come a time when you do doubt your purpose and your goal, especially if you don't see anybody else for a while. Sometimes I didn't even know if I was running on the right trail!

And yet six times during that race, I *was* paralyzed. You want to know what stopped me?

Pebbles in my shoes!

Can you imagine? There I was, running up a 14,110-foot piece of granite. But little pebbles were the biggest challenge I faced. I had to stop, take my shoes off, and take the pebbles out—six times! None of the other factors—the ones that made me so nervous—had had the effect of those tiny (but, all-powerful) little pieces of granite. Each and every time, I stopped and took the pebbles out. Failing to do so would have meant disaster! Ironic, isn't it? Accomplishing a goal of running up a 14,110-foot piece of granite and little pieces of that mountain stopped me!

~

When we spot pebbles in our lives, we have to be willing to remove them—not rationalize ourselves into believing that pebbles don't exist, or that they're a reason to stop moving forward altogether.

~

Pebble-Proofing

How many times in personal relationships, our careers, and our lives do we set our sights on some big goal and let some insignificant obstacle—something we can control easily if we want to—stand in our way?

You have a challenge. As you work your way through each of the exercises in this book, you will need to summon self-determination, purpose, and resolve to finish each one and move to the next one. You may be tempted to skip exercises. It may seem easier to let a "pebble" or two get in your way—and not finish the course. But don't let that happen. *Don't let a few pebbles take you out of the race!*

Take the pebbles out, and then keep going. Once you finish your course—the following chapters in this book—you'll begin to realize what using self-determination to harness the Power of Will can mean for you.

Build Your Foundation

I wrote this book for you… and for myself.

The way I see it, there really is no better way for me invest the past 50 years of my life (or to start the next 50) than to share with you everything of consequence that I know about personal growth. That's what's within these covers. This book is cause for a reevaluation of all of life's lessons—yours and mine—and for reacquaintance with the truth: remembering that even the most daunting challenges we face are always capable of bringing greater purpose to our lives.

Our visit here on planet earth is not long. Every once in a while we receive potent reminders of that fact. In my case, two shocking deaths brought greater purpose to my life in recent years and motivated me to try to live my life to its fullest, highest, and most correct dimensions. My mother, the greatest guiding light in my life, left for heaven in October 1992; my brother Al, my most valuable mentor and dearest friend, joined her, all too soon, in September 1995.

The loss of someone you cherish wakes you up like nothing short of a near-death experience. It motivates you to make the most of the precious time you've been given, to make conscious positive changes in your attitudes, your relationships, your career goals, the way you make financial decisions—everything. Losses like these, which are part of the human experience, either leave us permanently angry at the world or help us to understand and re-prioritize everything in life. The second option has been the best one for me.

Losing my mother and my brother reminded me of the old Italian proverb: "Our last garment is made without pockets." In other words, where we're going next, we won't be needing our car keys (or anything else, for that matter)! Fixating only on things you can actually stuff in a pocket, on things you can keep or hoard, is a little short-sighted.

My Aunt Rose shared that saying about the last garment with me many, many years ago. I still recall the occasion: She and my mom were making vestments for our neighborhood church. I was too young then to understand the real meaning, but I understand now, and if you've read this far in the book, you do, too.

Don't get distracted by small things you can put in your pockets. Don't wait to embrace the things that are truly valuable in life. There's no time for that. Start building your foundation today for a greater and more fulfilling life. (That's what this book is all about.) Find the time to be the best father, mother, brother, sister, or friend you can possibly be. Find the time to make a difference, find the time to love. Find the time to make yourself the person you were born to be, because that's the person who will be remembered. That's the person you want to be when you make your last and most important journey.

～ Chapter 2 ～

Practical Spirituality

How can you maintain a connection with the greatest power on earth—your own inner spirit? How can you get to truly know yourself? How should you share your gifts with others? These are important issues we'll examine in this chapter.

All Things Are Ready

Who we really are, how we should respond during crisis and success, and how we can best use our unique gifts are fundamental human concerns. Most physiological, inspirational, and religious systems tell us the answers we seek lie within.

I believe we must each find a way to connect with the limitless power resources available to our best and truest selves. Once we do, we can address virtually any challenge and win! This self-discovery is not self-absorption or ego-driven fantasy. It is humble, honest, internal development and discovery. It is the spiritual certainty leading to infinite possibility and simple fulfillment.

Four centuries ago, one of William Shakespeare's greatest heroes, Henry V, observed, "all things are ready if our minds be so." For Henry, spirituality joined seamlessly with an attitude of gratitude, a healthy, non-narcissistic understanding of self, and an unshakable firmness of purpose connecting him to his chosen mission. Shakespeare's king was a fictional character. It's true, though, that Henry's pragmatic approach to spirituality mirrored that of countless people who have since harnessed the Power of Will to enrich their lives. They have a clear sense of who they are (and who they're not); they celebrate the bounty a Higher Power has provided; and they know they have a responsibility to ready their minds for the purpose they've been placed on this earth to fulfill.

Poverty Comes in Many Forms

We tend to think of poverty as a lack of money or goods. Actually, the dictionary also defines the word poverty as "absence; a deficiency of necessary or desirable qualities." In this sense, unfortunately, spiritual poverty is rampant in our society.

You'll notice this lack of desirable spiritual qualities in some of the swankiest sections of most American cities (and plenty of other places). This spiritual bankruptcy shows itself most obviously as an absence of various qualities:

- 🏵 common courtesy
- 🏵 respect for the rights of others
- 🏵 caring for other people and wanting to help them succeed
- 🏵 genuine interest in making the world a better place to live
- 🏵 generosity and giving
- 🏵 adherence to the Golden Rule—"Do unto others as you would have them do unto you." (It was Benjamin Franklin who stated that this principle makes an excellent—and quite profitable—business philosophy. By the way, regardless of what you may have heard, I didn't learn this from Ben himself.)

Spiritual poverty is an epidemic in our society, as it is in many "developed" societies. I often wonder whether the absence of spiritual values is the most serious challenge we face in this country—it is far more serious than any economic, environmental, or public health crises. I've done a great deal of globetrotting in my life, and I've noticed a fascinating realization: it's the "rich" societies that seem to have the biggest problems with spiritual poverty, while the "poor" societies offer the real riches.

In countries where there is little to be shared, visitors are generally welcomed openly and eagerly—and, interestingly enough, usually offered a gift. In wealthier nations, there seems to be too much hoarding, jealousy, and destructive competitiveness, resulting in some spiritually degrading attitudes toward other people. I'm not saying that living in developed countries is bad, but I am saying that traveling to both developed and undeveloped countries yields surprising insights about the way people look at themselves, their possessions, and the possibility of connecting with other people.

In wealthy countries (like ours), the rich covet material objects they imagine they "own," and are likely to be deeply concerned about questions of status. When you meet wealthy people in developed countries, they are likely to begin conversations by asking where you live, what country club you belong to, what vehicle you drive, what you do for a living, or even the name of your plastic surgeon!

If you travel where poverty is the norm, however, you'll often find that new acquaintances are less interested in external considerations and where you rank in the hierarchy. They are more interested in what makes you a special person. They'll ask what you enjoy doing, what you find fulfilling, about your family, where your travels have taken you, what you've seen and tasted, and what has inspired you most in life. You can communicate with these people easily, even with language barriers. You share pictures, sing songs, learn traditional dances, and embrace all aspects of the other person's culture.

I ask you: Who is poor—and who is rich—in the above descriptions?

Years ago, I made a trip to Nepal, where the only "natural resources" to speak of are the spectacular mountain ranges of the Himalayas, and the extraordinary people. We ate dinner after a long day of trekking, relaxed by the fire, and sang and danced into the evening. A group of Sherpas shared a beautiful traditional wedding dance; my wife and I reciprocated with an impromptu performance of "Wooly Bully." What a powerful connection we all made with each other! And how little it had to do with status or cars or financial obsession, possessions or job titles! It had to do with who we all were, at a given moment in time.

I found myself thinking:

⁓

The greatest power and beauty is within.
Find it, harness it, show it unselfishly.

⁓

Discovering Ourselves—and Tapping into Our Inner Power

We must learn how to be ourselves, so we can tap into our own inner power. We must first accelerate our own journey to greater internal fulfillment—and gain the purposeful focus that comes from sound spiritual values. This purposeful focus, this sense of being oneself first, and a possessor of things second, is one of the hallmarks of the Power of Will.

Spiritual means "pertaining to the spirit or soul" or, if you prefer, pertaining to your true and pure mind. Spirituality connects us to our inner life and power. Once we truly understand who we are, then—and only then—can we make a serious attempt to understand the spirit, soul, mind, and the power of another person. In attempting to define ourselves with any honesty, we soon discover that we're not talking about our house, our cars, our furniture, our clothes, or our Gucci bags. We are talking about our essence as human beings.

There are countless systems for spiritual discovery, and I'm not going to try to summarize or pick among them. I do offer four simple steps to deepen your sense of connection with your Higher Power. These ideas are non-denominational and independent of concerns related to social stature, financial position, creed, or color. They can be used even by those who are uncomfortable discussing spiritual matters in conventional terms.

They are:

❀ Know yourself

❀ Be true to yourself

❀ Unselfishly share yourself with others

Let's look at each step in detail.

Step One: Know Yourself

One of the best ways to get to know yourself is to create a personal definition for who and what you really are. Get a big piece of paper and copy the basic form you see on the next page—which I call a Personal Value Inventory.

First, write your entire name on the top of the form (no initials allowed). If you're married and female please go the extra distance and add your maiden name.

Now you're going to create an "acronym" for your name! For each letter in your name, select a word that you feel accurately describes your values, qualities, personality traits, habits, and so on, most of the time. The key words here are "most of the time."

A gentle reminder: You aren't your stuff! Stay away from words that would describe a favorite hobby, your career, or any material possessions.

Rule number two is: Do this on your own. Take your time with this exercise; if you get stuck, use a dictionary or thesaurus. Under no circumstances, though, should you have anyone help you develop the words you associate with yourself. The point at this stage is to develop your own list of words.

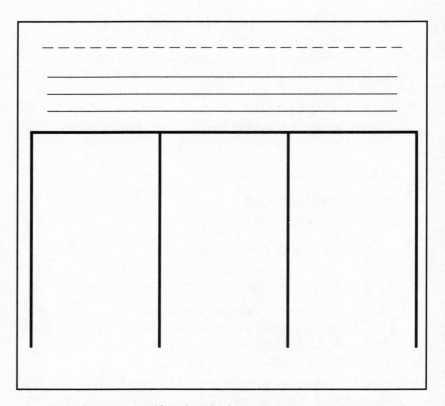

How do I see myself? Take a look at my acronym. I am Aggressive, Nurturing, Trustworthy, Honest, Overgenerous (that's usually a good thing), Nimble, Yes (I love the word "yes"), Forthright, Reckless, Altruistic, Non-conforming, Knowledgeable Purposeful, Affectionate, Reliable, Intuitive, Noble, Esteemed, Loyal, Lightheaded (no, wait, that's Lighthearted) and Optimistic. That's me—Anthony Frank Parinello!

Now take a close look at your acronym. Did you pick any words because you were stuck and couldn't think of a more appropriate one? If so, take a moment to remove them and think of some more meaningful words that define you. Discard words that you used for convenience or that don't realistically apply to you. Replace them with more appropriate words. Again—take your time!

~

I met someone yesterday... and much to my surprise,
it was me!

~

Once you're convinced that your acronym accurately reflects who you are, then share it with someone you trust—someone who knows you very well on a social or personal basis. This can be a best friend, a long-time acquaintance, a spouse, a significant other, or a companion. Under no circumstances should you change any of your words for the benefit of the person to whom you're showing the list! You're sharing this material for one reason and one reason only: to find out if your personal view of yourself is equivalent to what you project to others around you.

Highlight or circle any discrepancies.

This is not a test. You don't "fail" if there is disagreement or "pass" if there is total agreement. However, you should highlight, circle, or underline any words that are not in sync with this trusted person's opinion. After you have done this, take a clean copy of your acronym list to someone you work with who is not a friend but a peer. Once again, don't change any "mismatches," just highlight them in some way.

On the topic of "mismatches"—if you find that you have several, you'll need to pay close attention to the appropriate later chapters of the book, where we'll examine how to grow in particular areas.

Next, you're going to separate the words that you still feel make up your acronym into two different categories: Values/Beliefs and Qualities/Traits. Take a look at the form below; expand yours by adding the titles shown in the first two columns.

Values and beliefs form our social behavior; they are our core operating principles. If we compromise or deviate in the smallest way from our values and beliefs, we can usually count on short- or long-term negative consequences—perhaps even severe ones!

ANTHONY FRANK PARINELLO

Aggressive, Nurturing, Trustworthy, Honest, Overgenerous, Nimble, Yes, Forthright, Reckless, Altruistic, Nonconforming, Knowledgeable, Purposeful, Affectionate, Reliable, Intuitive, Noble, Esteemed, Loyal, Lighthearted, and Optimistic.

Values & Beliefs	Qualities & Traits	Gifts
Trustworthy	Aggressive	Nimble
Honest	Nurturing	Purposeful
Forthright	Overgenerous	
Loyal	Reliable	
Esteemed	Noble	
	Altruistic	
	Reckless	

Qualities and traits are characteristics that we may not always display under every circumstance. Qualities and traits can tolerate change. For instance, having a good sense of humor can be considered a quality or trait, rather than a value or a belief.

Although this is part of who you are, you may not always display this trait. Say that your cat just ate the center of your 200-year-old Persian rug, which had been in your family for five generations. People wouldn't be shocked or think you were acting out of character, if you didn't immediately chuckle and say, "Oh, well, it was 200 years old—and let's face it, nothing lasts forever."

Say that one of your values is being kind and good-natured to all creatures, and your actions are consistent with that value. If you were to have a screaming fit about all the ways you planned to punish the cat, you would probably confront feelings of regret and remorse after the fact. You might even be questioned (or ridiculed) by friends and family members for "overreacting" or acting in a way that "just isn't you."

Take a moment and separate your acronyms into these two distinct and different categories: Values/Beliefs and Qualities/Traits. If you feel uncertain about which word goes into a category, check my Personal Value Inventory (shown on the next page).

Step Two: Be True to Yourself

As a kid, one of my favorite songs was the Beach Boys' "Be True to Your School." Remember that one? It emphasized the importance of being loyal to one's "home team." It wasn't until I turned 50 that I realized the fundamental importance of being true—and I mean totally true—to your own "home team"—yourself. For many of us, that task is harder than it sounds. To some, it may seem selfish, perhaps too self-centered, and even inconsiderate. If you're experiencing any of those feelings, put them aside! You can (and must!) learn to be true to yourself, without compromising any relationships or feeling guilty.

The way I see it, being true to yourself means that you:

§ Seek the desires of your heart while being considerate of others.

§ Practice being non-judgmental.

ANTHONY FRANK PARINELLO

Aggressive, Nurturing, Trustworthy, Honest, Overgenerous, Nimble, Yes, Forthright, Reckless, Altruistic, Nonconforming, Knowledgeable, Purposeful, Affectionate, Reliable, Intuitive, Noble, Esteemed, Loyal, Lighthearted, and Optimistic.

Values & Beliefs	Qualities & Traits	Gifts
Trustworthy	Aggressive	Affectionate
Honest	Nurturing	Yes!
Forthright	Overgenerous	Optimistic
Loyal	Reliable	Lighthearted
Esteemed	Noble	Knowledgeable
Altruistic		
Nimble		
Reckless		
Purposeful		

Seek the Desires of Your Heart While Being Considerate of Others

At first glance, this seems simple: Do what your heart wants you to do. It's easy without a gap or obstacle, or if what your heart is telling you to do happens to be what you're already doing. When a gap exists between your heart's feelings and your thinking or actions, or when you face an external obstacle or conflict, then your heart and you have a challenge. What is the "right thing to do," anyway?

Let's say that your heart is telling you to relocate and change your environment. Your spouse, Janet, would love to move to Chicago. She loves sailing and the city life excitement, which seems an attractive break from your current laid-back lifestyle in Southern California. Your wife's sister lives in St. Charles, Illinois—close enough for the occasional visit, but not too close. You have no objections to this idea. In fact, after talking to your wife, you sometimes look forward to the change. After a little while, you're both talking about how moving to Chicago is the right thing to do.

Time to pack, right? Well, no. Among other things, you need to find a job, sell your condo, and find a way to finance the move. As the to-do list mounts, your brain has one of two reactions, and only one of them is in agreement with your heart. Your brain either gets excited about the challenges and starts moving in the direction of change and Chicago, or thinks about how much work making the move will entail and begins to rationalize why the move to Chicago should be put on hold for a while.

Sound familiar? Most of us have experienced an internal conflict like this from time to time. (We talked about this kind of push-me-pull-me conflict in the previous chapter.)

What to Do?

First, validate your heart's desire. Make sure it's "the real thing." Before you start packing—or doing anything else—ask yourself some questions:

1   Is this an original desire, or was it introduced by someone else's influence?

2   Were you emotionally susceptible at the time?

3   How long have you been carrying this desire in your heart?

4   Was there a time that you totally forgot about it? Partially forgot about it?

5   Have you genuinely experienced a small portion of this desire? If so, how did it feel?

6   What would happen to you (or others you care about who are involved in this situation) if you realized this desire and it turned out less satisfying than you had hoped? What would the emotional, financial and career consequences be?

7   If you could change this desire now to bring about a better coherence with your most cherished values, what would you change?

8   Will you be able to achieve this desire and still maintain prior or current promises to others you care about and/or who care about you?

9   Will you be able to achieve this desire and not compromise your core values, beliefs, qualities, and your purpose?

Using the example of the proposed move to Chicago, consider possible answers to these questions:

1   To be honest, it was really Janet's sister's idea, and that was because her sister brought it up during Christmas.

2   My emotional state was like a roller coaster, with the holidays and my favorite aunt's death just a few weeks later.

3   I've been thinking about making a change for two years.

4   Yes, I forgot about it just once, when I argued with my sister-in-law. I was thankful she was half a continent away! To be totally honest, I've never felt as strongly connected to this desire as Janet does.

5   Actually, we visited the area while on vacation. We've never considered the morning and evening commute.

6   If we made the move and it didn't work, it would be a financial disaster!

7   Well, I'd love it if my company would transfer me temporarily to Chicago. That way we could try it out without all of the financial, social, and emotional risks a permanent move would entail.

8   I did promise my boss that she'd be able to count on my involvement for the duration of the Johnson project, which is two years from completion. She would be disappointed, but it wouldn't cause grave damage to the project's outcome.

9   Yes, with one exception. One of my core values is that I am reliable and trustworthy. My boss wouldn't see it that way.

This process could help your heart, you, and your partner to arrive at a mutually satisfactory outcome—you lobby for a transfer so you can both experiment with Chicago living without selling your home or making a full-time work commitment.

Getting Your Mind to Take Action on Your Heart's Desire

Let's say you have asked yourself the nine questions, and the process makes you more certain about your heart-driven objective. You've confirmed that you do have a strong desire to take action in a certain area. You've validated your desire; you're ready to talk your mind into action. It's time to take action and make it a reality.

  ❀ First, ask yourself: Do I currently have any limitations that would make this desire unreachable? What can I do about changing these limitations? Are there any that cannot be changed? Can I change my perception about any of the unchangeable limitations, so they can be viewed as an asset to achieving this desire?

Not all limitations are bad. Some can help you. Say that Janet is single and wants to move to Chicago, but she lacks enough money to move. She asks for a raise and starts saving instead of spending. In one year, she has enough money and a new job in Chicago at a higher salary, due, in part, to her recent raise and boost in salary history.

❀ Next, develop your commitment to doing what you believe is right. Take small steps first; build your confidence in your desire. Remember, the Power of Will takes the form of single-minded attention! Read all you can about your desire; become educated about your objective. You need clarity and confidence to take action on something you believe deeply.

Suppose Janet becomes a Chicago expert. She reads about the city's history and subscribes to the daily newspaper. Although she lives in a different city, she feels like a Windy City resident before she arrives—and she has great leads for vacant apartments!

❀ Investigate each step you'll take. Examine how you've taken other heartfelt desires and made them reality. Identify individuals who can help achieve this objective. Ask for help; explain exactly why you feel you're doing *the* right thing.

If you can, identify someone who has realized similar desires. Does this person agree that you're doing the right thing? If so, is this person willing to act as a coach or mentor? If not, what concerns or questions should you have taken into account previously?

❀ Expect confusion, setbacks, and complications. Avoid anything that may sabotage your efforts to translate what your heart wants into reality. Keep your "eyes on the prize"—and don't sell yourself short or talk yourself down. Focus positively and constantly on what you know to be a moral and personal right. Give yourself time— and learn from—setbacks.

I believe, in many cases, that following your heart is similar to running a marathon. You must work your way up to the goal. On your very first day of training, it is certainly not a good idea to attempt a 20-mile run! As you build strength, you must eat right, take vitamins, and use the right equipment. Yet, if the night before your marathon, you abuse your body with excessive alcohol or other nasty substances, you are guaranteed failure in your quest.

It is the same when turning what your heart wants into reality. Replace negative self-talk with enabling convictions, and watch for early signs of self-defeating attitudes. Don't sabotage yourself by replaying outside influences that are not in your best interest. Remember my Pike's Peak experience? You need total self-determination to avoid any influence inside (or outside) your head that negates your heart's desire. Remove the pebbles and push on! Take small steps every single day toward your heart's goal, and for each step you take, reward yourself.

- Finally, ask yourself: "What can I do to strengthen the Values/Beliefs and Qualities/Traits necessary to make this desire a reality?" Once you validate your heart's objective, check your list of Values/Beliefs and Qualities/Traits. Reorder the list. Which ones will you need to develop further in order to make your heart's desire a reality? Begin to strengthen each of these areas.

I know it's difficult to apply exact procedures to make your heart's desires a reality. But the steps I've outlined will provide a "starter's checklist" for you.

Be Non-judgmental

Are you like me? Do you just hate it when someone judges you and your values, actions, and behavior? Isn't that irritating? I always think: What gives them the right to say what's correct or incorrect about what I do? That's a despicable habit! People who pass judgment on me—all of them —are pitiable, morally challenged creatures. They're a menace! In fact, judgmental types are such a danger to the American way of life that they should each have their lips welded to the nearest toxic waste processing plant outlet and made to…

Well, never mind.

It's easy to play judge and jury. Every time I catch myself becoming judgmental about someone's behavior, I ask myself these two questions:

- Do I have any sympathy for this person or situation?
- Am I showing any empathy for this person or situation?

There is a big difference between sympathy and empathy. Having sympathy is feeling almost exactly as someone else is feeling by actively participating in emotions of joy, grief, disappointment, and so on. On the other hand, being empathetic is having an intellectual and/or emotional understanding of how someone else is feeling and holding that understanding in high regard. In other words, you may never *feel* the joy or grief, fortune or misfortune of the other person, but you do *understand* it.

I will probably never be able to have sympathy for parents, immigrants, criminals, movie stars, or world class athletes! I'm not in any of those categories, and I don't have any direct experience with their challenges. It is easy for me to empathize with all of these people because I have become an expert listener. Expert listening is the fastest way to develop empathy—and to put the Golden Rule into practice, not theory.

Let's face it—listening is important! We all want to be heard. When you truly listen to someone, you're treating that person as you'd like to be treated. That's exactly why:

～

Our creator gave us two ears and only one mouth!

～

Here is my Top-Ten List of action steps to becoming a non-judgmental, expert empathetic listener:

10 As you listen, continually ask yourself: "Why is this person telling/asking me this?"

9 As you listen, ask yourself: "Does this person's body language match what he/she is saying/asking?"

8 As you listen, ask yourself: "What are the most important words this person is saying?"

7 As you listen, ask yourself: "What is this person feeling right now?" Important note: Don't fall into the listening trap of asking yourself why the person might be feeling a certain way. This is a sure-fire way to become judgmental without even knowing it!

6 As you listen, don't interrupt! Let the other person speak his/her mind and complete his/her thought. However, it is a good idea to offer brief supportive words as he/she speaks and you listen.

5 If, as you listen, the other person becomes stuck and starts mentally searching for a word, wait it out! Don't offer the word; resist the temptation to "help." Even if uncomfortable, let the other person come up with his or her own words at the pace that makes the most sense.

4 As you listen, resist all temptation to let your mind move too far ahead of the conversation. Don't think about what you're going to say next, but remain focused on what the other person is saying.

3 As you listen, maintain a gentle eye contact. Don't stare, but don't let anything or anyone distract you. A good listening attitude reflects genuine interest in what the other person is saying.

2 As you listen, stay in the moment. Don't let your mind wander to irrelevant subjects or daydreams of other places and people (i.e., "I think I should be cleaning out my sock drawer").

1 As you listen, remember that your mind processes information about eight times faster than the average person talks. It is easy to get ahead of somebody and to start preparing responses before he or she has finished a sentence. Be patient. Hear the other person out, and resist all temptation to speak before the other person is ready. When you do speak, say something that shows you have been listening before you change the subject. ("That's a fascinating story! It reminds me of the time I went down the Colorado rapids...")

Step Three: Unselfishly Share Yourself with Others

The best way to share yourself with others is to live a rich and full life that comes from internal satisfaction, from knowing that you're showing unique gifts to people and the world at large.

The fastest way to discover your unique gifts and how to share them is to go back to our Personal Value Inventory form. Label the third column "Gifts," as I have done to mine, shown on the next page.

Take a minute to select from your list the values and traits you feel have been directly responsible for your greatest success and enjoyment. Everyone has experienced success, fulfillment, and victory. Think about events in life for which you are most grateful right now.Which of your unique gifts had a greater impact on making things happen? Take a moment right now and copy your most prevalent Values/Beliefs and Qualities/Traits to the Gifts column on your form.

You may realize that you possess special unique gifts in addition to the ones within your values, beliefs, qualities, and traits. Amplify these elements in the unique gifts column of your Personal Value Inventory form.

As you can see, one of the gifts that I display when I am successful or totally enjoying myself is my sense of humor. I share this gift when I am at my best. What is at the top of your list of gifts? How often do you show these gifts?

ANTHONY FRANK PARINELLO

Aggressive, Nurturing, Trustworthy, Honest, Overgenerous, Nimble, Yes, Forthright, Reckless, Altruistic, Nonconforming, Knowledgeable, Purposeful, Affectionate, Reliable, Intuitive, Noble, Esteemed, Loyal, Lighthearted, and Optimistic.

Values & Beliefs	Qualities & Traits	Gifts
Trustworthy	Aggressive	Affectionate
Honest	Nurturing	Yes!
Forthright	Overgenerous	Optimistic
Loyal	Reliable	Lighthearted
Esteemed	Noble	Knowledgeable
Altruistic	Nonconforming	
Nimble	Intuitive	
Reckless		
Purposeful		

You can summon your gifts and share them with others anytime you choose. All you have to do is revisit a "high point" that you strongly associate with one of your gifts.

Let me explain. I have worked in sales most of my professional life. Sales have ups and downs—the peaks can be extremely high, and the valleys can be extremely low! When I experience a high, I energize all my senses to totally enjoy and prolong the moment. I benefit even more from my hard work to get to that point.

There is also a hidden benefit. When I am in a low period of energy and performance, and eager to bring my business relationship with another person up a notch or two to make that sale, I recall my emotional high—and share the gifts with the other person! This shift in attitude may be brief, but long enough for me to put any interaction in perspective. I do this with the assistance of my five senses: sound, sight, taste, touch, and smell.

Consider the following true story. One of my greatest moments in sales came when I received the Most Valuable Player of the Year award from my employer. That was the year I achieved 150 percent of my plan! The MVP award itself is a four-foot high "perpetual trophy," but the recognition that comes with that trophy is what really registered for me. This was the highest award the company gave—and they'd given it to me!

I can clearly remember everything about the awards banquet. It was at the Pointe, a posh resort in Phoenix, Arizona. The MVP award is given last and there are only one or two senior level officials who know the identity of the award recipient. I was sitting with five of my peers. We had just finished dinner; I was sipping vanilla nut coffee. The waiters and waitresses were picking up the dishes; the lights were dimmed but the stage was bright as day. When the announcer said: "The winner of this year's MVP award is Tony Parinello," everybody at my table turned and looked at me. The crowd began to roar, and I jumped to my feet. As I ran to the stage, people began to stand, giving me "thumbs-up" and "high-fives." It was a great feeling!

I looked into the audience, bright lights shining in my face. I felt the dryness in my throat that comes with drinking coffee and was nervous when I said: "Being ahead of quota is great, but this..." (holding the trophy with both hands over my head) "this is grand!" Then I called several people to the stage, people who had been an integral part of my team and made my success possible. Together, we carried that trophy off the stage. What a night!

Here's the point. Because that particular moment in time is wired into a permanent part of my memory with each of my five senses, I can recall it anytime I want. It sometimes jumps into my mind without even trying! The other day I walked past an espresso bar and I happened to smell vanilla nut coffee brewing. I instantly thought of my MVP trophy! What's fascinating is that I not only thought of my trophy, but I smiled and I actually saw the faces of the peers who happened to be sitting at the table with me that memorable night. About five minutes after I had walked past the espresso bar, I pumped some coins into a pay phone to make a business call. When it was time to speak, my throat was dry, just the way it was when I'd tried to express my joy into that microphone.

Why not recreate your success to share your gifts with others anytime you want? The truth is, we have all used our gifts to attain some kind of success (such as a favor!) at points in our lives, although we may not have been totally aware of the success at the time. There are several possible reasons for this.

First, we may have been focused on a bigger result and failed to see the smaller accomplishments as important. This happens all the time, often because of conditioning we received as children. Did you know that by the time we reach 18, most of us have heard the word "no" or some variation 148,000 times? It's no wonder that we're not automatically conditioned to recognize or acknowledge our smaller accomplishments! What does that mean? It means we have to make a conscious effort to "hard-wire" those moments when we felt the greatest joy, exhilaration, and gratitude, so we can replay them for our benefit and the benefit of others when the need arises.

The more sensory involvement we bring to our "gift" moment, the more powerful the experience will be, and the more likely your gift will repeat with little or no effort. When hitting a high point in life, use all five senses to "burn in" the moment. You'll be able to reexperience that exact gift, and share it with others, anytime you want.

Here's an example using my second gift: humor. The following is a list of the conditions that exist in my five senses when I am at my funniest:

- ❀ *Sight*: I actually see hundreds of people laughing at one of my anecdotes.
- ❀ *Sound*: I actually hear ongoing chatter long after the laughter has stopped. "He's really funny..." "Oh, what a character..."
- ❀ *Taste*: I taste apple juice. I always drink a glass of apple juice when I give my presentations. Why? It has no after-taste and coats my throat. It looks like scotch, which I turn into a prop for one of my jokes!
- ❀ *Touch*: I feel the metal of a hand-held microphone. I also have to be standing up.
- ❀ *Smell*: I smell an audience! It's an interesting blend of perfume and cologne—a pleasant odor, and never offensive.

The other day, I was discouraged about an important business contact that wasn't returning my calls. I needed success. I needed this person to call me. I had left several messages about the importance of scheduling time to talk. Finally, I thought, "Let me use one of my greatest gifts. I'll use my sense of humor to get a response." So I recalled all of the five senses above. I saw, heard, tasted, touched, and smelled, then I stood up as I reached for the phone, called his voice mail number, and left him this message: "Mr. So-and-so, every night before I go to bed I talk to God. Why can't I talk to you?"

He returned my call within 15 minutes—and he was in a great mood! You just can't argue with recalling your best gift, and using every one of your senses to show it!

The Right Recipe

I love lasagna. I consider myself an expert on lasagna. Not making it—eating it. I often order it when I am on the road, always comparing taste and flavor and the way different layers are assembled. You might say I am searching for the world's best lasagna!

I'm not sure, but I imagine there must be over 200 different recipes for lasagna—yet, the ingredients are basically the same: tomato paste and puree, garlic, olive oil, chopped parsley, oregano, basil, and so on. Why then, does one person's lasagna taste so much better than another's? You might answer that it's in the quality and freshness of each ingredient.

Okay, let's narrow this down a bit. You can't argue with quality; it's sure to have an impact on the taste. Nevertheless, take two identical recipes that use the exact same ingredients and have two different people follow the recipe to a "T." From my personal experience, I know the chances are good that one will taste better.

Why? I believe there are three reasons:

- The cook's attention to detail
- The accuracy of the cook's five senses
- The cook's passion to make the best lasagna

Similarly, all three of these elements must be present when we try to "cook up" a gift related to a past success. We must follow predetermined steps. We must also be careful as we carry out the steps, being sure to fully engage our senses, and carry out the job with great passion!

With that warning in mind, write the recipe for your greatest success. You'll be able to recall any gift you have when you need it, and you'll use the most powerful recipe you know. Copy onto a piece of paper the recipe form you see on the next page:

Make enough copies so you'll be able to write each one of your gifts on a separate sheet. Give each one a heading: "My favorite recipe for..."

Concentrate. I suggest a quiet place with no distracting noise or interruptions. Take your first gift. Recall a time and place where you displayed this gift with a favorable impact, like in the above paragraph when I recalled the gift of humor. Close your eyes and relive the experience in great detail. Try to recall feelings using all your senses. Once recalled, write down two or

My Recipe for:

_____

What I See: _____

What I Hear: _____

What I Smell: _____

What I Feel : _____

What I Say: _____

What I Think: _____

three words that describe what you heard, what you saw, what you tasted, what you said, and what scent(s) you were able to smell and so on.

Get the details right! Remember, the more descriptive your words, the more powerful your recall. You're looking for a *vivid* memory of the event in question. When I needed to powerfully deliver my voice-mail message, I pictured the audience, heard their comments, tasted the apple juice, got a whiff of the perfume and cologne, and bingo! I delivered one of the best voice mail messages in my career! I was "on"—I was doing what I do best, what I was meant to do.

You can share the same kind of gift in your life—anytime you need to!

A Sense of Openness, a Sense of Purpose

Opening up to the world around you is one of the most practical, accessible forms of spirituality. This seemingly simple practice reminds you, at a fundamental level, of whom you truly are.

Some people are better at it than others—but we can all benefit from a more observant life approach.

Not long ago, I was out for a run. I had a lot to do that morning, but I felt it was important to put in some miles and to clear my head from a hectic week of travel, speeches, and deadlines. I live in a small town, about 50 miles east of downtown San Diego. Highway 78 goes through our quaint two-block-long "town"— picturesque, almost all the buildings have been restored from the old California Gold Rush days. It's a quiet town. The sidewalks roll up (or might as well) at about 7:00 P.M. Actually, the only sidewalks we have happen to line this two-block area. The rest is unpaved, which could represent a problem for the physically challenged. Unless, of course, that person happens to be my friend Dave.

Dave has lived in our town for 25 years. He is blind. He lives on Highway 78 and, to go into town to shop, he must navigate the shoulders of the highway as cars whiz past. The drivers must be as amazed as I am every time I see Dave walking to town, as sure and safe as anyone with full eyesight.

Well, on this cold but beautiful Saturday morning, as I ran up the hill on 78 toward town, Dave walked along with a plastic bag in one hand and his red-tipped cane in the other. As I approached him, I said, "Good morning, Dave, it's Tony coming up behind you." He said "Oh, yeah, I heard you for some time now. This hill's a killer isn't it?" (It's funny, but I bet anyone who saw me, but didn't take the time to hear me, would not have known that I labored going up that hill!)

"Where are you headed, Dave?"

"To the library," he said, "I've got to bring back these tapes."

I slowed to a fast walk, impressed at Dave's fast pace. "Yeah, it's a bit of a challenge to cross over the highway. There aren't very many landmarks on the other side to help me to find the entrance to the library."

Taking the opportunity to walk for a while, I offered to assist in his crossing. We walked and talked, and I noticed how Dave would swing his cane from the asphalt to the dirt, keeping his left foot on the dirt and his right one on the asphalt, safely inside the solid white line of the shoulder. We reached the place where we had to cross the highway, and Dave held my arm. As we crossed the center line, I tripped on one of the small reflectors glued to the roadway.

"Be careful," Dave said, "I don't want to have to pick you up!"

After we deposited the tapes at the library, I asked where Dave wanted me to drop him off so he could get his bearings.

"At the drugstore, if you don't mind," he said. "I've got to pick up a prescription."

This was no problem in a small town. We talked about his ham radio and the world news. As we approached the corner drug-store, I placed Dave's hand on the railing. "Here you go, Dave," I said. His response gave me an entirely new perspective on my ability to see.

"This isn't the right entrance to the drugstore," he said.

"What?"

Dave's next response gave me chills. "This is the entrance to the café," he said. "The entrance I need is the pharmacy."

I was amazed, looking up the short five steps to the door. Sure enough, it was the cafe's entrance.

"Here, let me show you," said Dave. He took my arm and, with his cane, brought me over to the second entrance, which looked like the first one. "This is the pharmacy."

"Wait a minute," I said. "I've got eyes and I couldn't see that it was the wrong entrance. How could you tell?"

"Put your hand on this railing." I did as he instructed. "Now, go to the other entrance and put your hand on it and feel the difference."

I walked over and felt the other railing. "I don't feel any difference."

"Do it again," he suggested.

And that time I did feel it! Although both railings looked identical from above, under one there was a small weld, while the other was ground smooth.

"That's how you can tell," said Dave. "You can also hear the dishes being moved about in the café. Listen."

Dave started to climb the stairs to the pharmacy. "Tony, be careful on your run home. Watch where you're going. The highway is busy on weekends."

As I ran home—carefully—I thought: "How many times have I looked without seeing?"

The world we live in is an extraordinary place. Strive to open yourself up to it completely!

I came away from that discussion with Dave vowing never to "look for" anything again without at least trying to use my other four senses. I know that I take too many of the gifts my maker has given me for granted. Do you? I know that I need to add more observation, more passion, and more involvement to every aspect of my life. Do you? I know that if I put my mind to it, I can start to use all of my senses to gain a fuller appreciation of, and show more gratitude to the country and world where I have been placed.

How about you?

Catalog What's Important

What do you take for granted? Health, love, reputation, money, freedom? How would your life change if one of these were suddenly and without warning taken away and removed from your life?

It sometimes takes a massive wake-up call to summon us to action, to make us realize what items should be at or near the top of our "to do" list... and what items shouldn't be. Often, we're tempted to define happiness and success in terms of objects and possessions. We need to stop and ask ourselves: What's really important in life? Before you go on in this book, apply that question to your own life, and see what answers you come up with. Is that which is important to you an inanimate object, a possession, a position in a hierarchy—or is it your relationship with someone who loves you, or to a Higher Power? Then you might ask yourself: How much of my time and energy is devoted to that which is truly important to me?

Your spirit, as invisible as it is, will show its power every time you ask it to. You can always request your own wake-up call, and, with the help of a Higher Power, you can always find a way to focus in more meaningfully on those parts of your life that support your best and highest self. So, wake yourself up—in the way that's best for you—and look around. Do you prefer music or a buzzer for your wake-up call?

~ Chapter 3 ~

Understanding Yourself and Others

How Well Do You Know Yourself?

Talk about a big question! Let's break it down into smaller components. How do you get motivated? What do you do when you're tempted to procrastinate about something important? Do you tend toward an internal or external measurement of your world? And how well do you understand your own personality traits and those of other people?

In this chapter, you'll learn how to motivate yourself effectively. You'll discover your personality type and predisposition when it comes to evaluating the outside world. You'll learn how to increase your constructive processing of outside influences, which likely will lead to harmonious relationships with others.

"*If It Bleeds, It Leads*"

Anyone watching CNN or scanning the *New York Times* knows the world can be complex and scary.

Nations always arm themselves to the teeth, preparing for (or launching) wars against neighbors. Poverty, suffering, tragedy, and betrayal always seem to be part of the most important new developments. If you're like me, when you go to sleep at night, you sometimes wonder what awful events will be news the next day! Producers and editors often seem to enjoy news that will "shock" and "disturb" us—following the old maxim, "If it bleeds, it leads."

If people do favors for each other, and mend quarrels, or have purposeful, optimistic dreams or stare silent and bewitched by the eyes of a baby; or find any reason to give thanks for the gift of life, we never seem to read about it on the front page of the newspaper, or hear about it when we flip on the television or radio.

Conflict, danger, discord, and pain make the biggest headlines on the local, national, and international levels; perhaps because we respond with an attentive, deeply rooted defensive reflex to conflict, danger, and discord in our own lives. Let's face it: It's easy for people to get bent out of shape over one thing or another; it can often seem quite difficult to understand your next door neighbor, spouse, or significant other.

Are human beings really meant not to understand each other? Or have we taught ourselves to lose sight of opportunities to interact harmoniously with others?

Whether we try to figure out what's going on inside someone else's head, or why the city council voted down a bill meant to improve local schools, or even why the world economy is in bad shape, I believe we'll have an easier time if we learn some basic human behavior principles. When we understand what really drives another person or group, we may comprehend the occasional interpersonal flare-ups in our corner of the universe, and perhaps avoid being manipulated quite so shamelessly by the flare-ups in a state, a continent, or half a world away. And here's the best part: To learn what motivates others, we must learn what motivates us! Once we figure out how to motivate ourselves, we'll be in a better position to interact effectively with other people.

Decades of industrial and behavioral research conducted with real people in real workplaces who had real families has yielded some remarkable tools. I want to discuss some of these tools in this chapter and help you use them in your relationships and with yourself.

After half a century of learning through direct experience encompassing so many joys and sorrows, I can vouch for the principles in this chapter. They're good science—and practical resources for your immediate benefit, even when your world seems a little crazy. You can use the ideas and principles we'll be discussing to do the following:

- Take conscious control of what motivates you.

- Learn what goes into good decisions—and, just as important, what's likely to lead to bad decisions—once you're motivated.

- Identify and update the way you look at "the world at large."

- Find out about the four main personality types and figure out how to use what you know about them to improve your relationships.

Why Do We Do What We Do?

Like many motivational speakers, I've done my share of research, formal and informal, on questions like "What makes people tick?" and "How do you motivate someone?" There are lots of competing and compelling strategies for getting and staying motivated, but I believe there is only *one* potentially constructive motivator. Unfortunately, it bears the same initials as one of the most feared departments of our federal government—the ultimate negative motivator, you might say.

This motivating force is the famous IRS, Internally Relating to the Situation.

How you relate internally to a situation determines how you address any—repeat any—interpersonal challenge or motivational roadblock, even one that involves a showdown with someone or something as fearsome as the other IRS.

How you relate internally to any situation always determines the degree and kind of motivation you experience. This reation affects decisions you make. These decisions determine the degree to which you recognize in your own life that you are the ultimate authority figure. These decisions determine the amount of power you grant to outside forces seeking to control your actions.

You can attend all the seminars, read all the books, listen to all of the audiotapes, see all the posters of a solitary mountain climber standing on a pinnacle, and watch coaches yell and scream as athletes bang heads or slap backsides all night long. But when it comes down to it, you and I and everyone else on earth are identical in two key areas: We're naturally motivated by internal associations we make to one of two forces.

People call these two forces Reward or Penalty, the Carrot and the Stick, Pain or Pleasure, Retreat or Advancement, and any number of names. You can say them any way you like, there are always just two of them. ("Clean up your room—and I'll give you a lollipop!" "Clean up your room—or you won't be able to sit down for a week!") The world is full people trying to convince us they'll push our pleasure buttons, or pound on our pain buttons, if we act in certain ways. In final analysis, the way *we* choose to relate internally to each situation, and the degree *we* associate pain or pleasure with a given action, determines the level and quality of our motivation.

Our IRS Tendencies

It would be wonderful if we always instinctively choose the internal relationship in a given situation that is most constructive and most supportive to our internal growth. Unfortunately, it doesn't always happen that way.

As I see it, we all tend to look first and perhaps only at the immediate penalty or reward, pain or pleasure, retreat or advancement—and, for who knows what reason, we usually focus on the negative implications we face. Our motivation seem to come from what's going to happen right now, or in a short time, rather than what may be possible in the future. We seem to focus on the worst possible outcome, rather than the best possible outcome.

Fortunately, though this initial tendency exists, we control our minds. We can—and should—learn to translate any incoming stimulus into a motivation linked to reward, pleasure, and advancement. We can—and should—learn to think in the long term.

Let me give you a real life example. In 1982, my sales manager put me on probation. I was given six months to get back in the swing of things—or find another place to work! At the time, I was at a dismal 19 percent of quota; in hindsight, I realize that my actions (or lack of) gave my manager little choice but to put me on probation. That may have been the right thing for my manager to do, but I realize now that what wasn't right was the way I responded.

I let my manager "motivate" me by targeting my fear of job loss. I responded with all the stress, acid indigestion, social embarrassment, worry, and outright panic that losing one's job would bring. I lived that painful outcome before it actually happened.

Well, as it turned out, I saved my job, but I nearly went nuts, too. My friends told me I aged by a decade or more in that six-month period! (I like to think I've won some of those "lost years" back in the intervening time.)

Six years after that probation scare, I left that company and the manager behind, and started my own company, which is based on the principles I used to get business when the chips were down. Those ideas led to a book that, wonder of wonders, sold lots and lots of copies!

The essence of both the business and the book was "How to Get Appointments with Very Important Top Officers." I ended up teaching skills and tactics I developed and used to get off probation and earned a lot of money as a result. Once on my own, I realized how much time and energy I had wasted being terrified of the dreaded "pink" slip. Sure, I'd been motivated to find a new way of doing things. But if I had translated the stimulus properly, relating internally to the situation as an opportunity for long-term reward rather than immediate punishment, I would have avoided the paralyzing fear and panic about my probation. What's more, I could have:

1   Looked upon my probation as a positive opportunity to learn and advance—and, thanks to a few less sleepless nights, developed my new appointment-getting techniques much sooner.

2   Avoided subtracting 12 years from my life.

3   Written my book much sooner.

4   Started my own business—and built it into a success— much sooner!

If, instead of allowing myself to feel terrified, I had asked myself, "What can I learn from this situation—and how can I put it to my benefit immediately?" I could have had a much different experience. I honestly believe I would have saved myself a good deal of self-imposed heartache and terror.

Every negative motivating emotion is self-imposed. And every positive motivating emotion is self-imposed, too. We can choose what we want.

This isn't a play on words, or a reversal of what's important, or a denial of basic emotional realities. With practice, you really can learn to relate internally to any situation in precisely the way you choose. Once you realize that fear really does make good results harder, and once you build up enough IRS "muscle" to choose positive rather than negative rewards—you call the shots! You choose the motivating forces driving your responses— not your boss, the media, or your surly brother-in-law.

At this point in life, I've learned to relate internally to situations in such a way that virtually none of my day-to-day activities are motivated by fear. And you know what? Life is a whole lot better now!

Today, no matter how daunting the challenge, I look hard at every situation and ask the following questions:

- What can I gain from this?
- What advance can I make as a direct result of this situation?
- How can I turn this into a victory for me and everyone else?

Usually, thanks to the magic of repetition, I get answers that help me relate internally to a situation in a way that gets me hooked up to an attractive potential reward, and not a terrifying potential penalty. Does it take practice to respond to challenging situations with these questions? Sure. But that practice has paid off in higher self-esteem, increased energy, and exciting financial rewards!

The Moral

The bottom line for motivation is clear: Decisions we make to cling to short-term fear or focus on long-term pleasure have a tremendous effect on the quality of our lives. I'm certainly not alone in this position. Virtually every respected industrial and behavioral scientist agrees that management by fear simply doesn't work.

Managers, parents, clergy, you and I—and anyone who encourages others to do their best—should learn to congratulate and praise rather than pounce and criticize. We'll get more out of people when they discuss positive traits in detail and envision problems as transitional situations on the way to something better. Whether the people who interact with you do this or not, the challenge is always to manage yourself effectively.

"Easy to say, Parinello—but the world I live in doesn't always play that way! People have a funny way of asking me to focus on things other than my own emotional state—and of emphasizing the negative outcomes I may experience if I don't perform up to their expectations!" True enough. That's all the more reason for you to assume conscious control of the way you internally relate to situations. Learn to move past fear, pain, and loss motivators of the present—instead, look to pleasure, joy, gain, and future advancement and possibilities. Every single event that happens today, bar none, can be turned into future benefit investment—if you make IRS decisions to your best advantage and make a constant, silent habit of asking yourself these questions: "What is this person's motivation? Do they operate from fear or pleasure?" "How can I make this situation turn out positively for everyone involved?" "What can I learn from this?"

Facing a challenging situation? Here are some questions you can use to find out relevant details about someone's motivation:

§ Is this person acting on emotion or logic? Fact or conjecture?

§ Will this person derive any tangible result (i.e., monetary gain or the receipt of a desired object or emotion) from this action?

§ Does this person want you to win or lose?

§ If this person wins, will you lose? If this person loses, will you win?

§ Does this person respect you? Can you find something you respect about this person?

You can use these questions to move closer to the goal of making every situation a pleasurable one for everyone involved.

§ What can you give that would make the other party feel good—and what would it cost you to give it?

§ Would the outcome change in intensity if each party felt better about the exchange?

Is there any way to provide greater value for the other party? Is it possible for you to go the extra distance in this situation?

You can use these questions to learn from virtually any experience you encounter:

§ What aspects of your life could be positively affected by this experience?

§ Where else could you use this information or experience?

§   How can you make your senses summon up a mindset that prevailed when you developed a solution to a similar challenge?

When you need reinforcement on this score, just remind yourself: "No one ever gets out of here alive." We only have so much time on earth. This moment is too precious to spend in a state of panic or fear—and, with practice, you learn not to waste energy building up those unproductive emotions. With practice, you learn to make your decision regarding how you will relate internally to the situation in a way that envisions positive outcomes, increased knowledge, and success in the long term.

Two Kinds of Decisions

Once you've evaluated your situation correctly and internally committed yourself to derive long-term positive value from it, you're going to have to make decisions. There's a lot to be said about the different decision-making styles, and you'll get more insight on that (complex) topic a little later in the book. For now, let's consider the driving forces behind every decision: *choice and necessity.*

Decisions driven by *choice* are most likely to be successful for everyone involved—including you! In the choice scenario, you look at all the options, and, motivated by your own goals, choose what's right for you. Everyone has a unique decision-making style, and some people feel more comfortable with rapid decisions. But the point of choice-driven decisions is that you don't have to make a quick decision *unless you feel like it*. You've got time to evaluate all the factors, and you're less likely to waste key resources like time, money, happiness, and health.

Decisions driven by *necessity* are also common, but that doesn't mean they're fun! These are situations when you have few or no appealing options; your back is or could be up against the wall. When you feel forced into a situation, when you choose the lesser of two evils, and when you "have no choice"—you're facing a necessity-driven decision.

Actually, these two decision-making scenarios are connected. Everything in life is a choice before it's a necessity. If we choose not to make a choice, we will eventually enter the World of Necessity. I can't think of any exception to this rule.

Let me provide an example. Recently, a certified letter from the Internal Revenue Service arrived at our office. One of my team members looked at it; her heart skipped a beat. She handed it to another team member, who brought it to me and said, nervously, "Tony, I've got a registered letter from the IRS here." I tried to lighten the mood by smiling and saying, "Maybe it's a check!"

As it turned out, it wasn't a check, but it was a demand that I garnish the wages of an employee for failing to pay his back income tax! How did this state of affairs come about? Well, that employee's choice back in 1992 not to pay his income tax created a chain of events that resulted in a classic necessity situation. The IRS had garnished his wages, and I had no choice but to comply if I wanted to keep my company within the law—which I did. That initial choice in 1992 also created two other necessities—a non-negotiable $900 penalty, and the non-negotiable requirement that my employee pay all his debts off at a time when he was strapped for cash.

In this case, as in any other case, *The choice we fail to make leads us to the necessity decision.* For my employee, as for the rest of us, the mother of the necessity decision was that familiar hindrance known as procrastination.

The truth is we all procrastinate, whether we admit it or not. Have you ever put off acting on a dream or idea? Have you ever "forgotten" about a visit to the dentist for your regular check-up and cleaning? If so, you've procrastinated. For the most part, casual, infrequent occurrences of procrastination in low-risk areas are no big deal, especially if we eventually follow through on the item. However, if delays, excuses, and postponements show up on a regular basis and lead to a profusion of necessity-decision situations in critical areas, we've got a problem! We've built up an unhealthy pattern, often without even realizing we were doing so.

Let's assume that doing the dishes or taking out the trash is not one of your favorite chores. Let's also assume that the person you happen to be sharing your life and living quarters with is a "neatnik." At the beginning of the relationship, the first time you delayed cleaning up, maybe a few words were exchanged. But on the next two or three occasions, "Mr. or Ms. Clean" decided it was simpler to handle all the cleanup. You may have gotten a cross look or two, but your brain got the message: "I'm off the hook." In fact, you were rewarded for not doing your job. That built up a pattern! You stopped thinking about doing the dishes or taking out the trash—and you took your partner's efforts for granted.

The problem? Suppose your partner's steadily increasing resentment over having to handle the cleanup chores builds and builds over days, weeks, months, and possibly years... until, one day, the dam breaks. Your partner is angry. Your partner has had enough. Your partner perceives this problem as a symbol of neglect in key relationship areas. Gulp! You've now got no choice but to try to focus in on the issue and try to change a (now deeply ingrained) pattern of behavior—one that may have led you to take your partner for granted in other areas.

If you and I don't want to face the serious consequences of life's "late fees"—that is to say, if we don't want to be "backed into" the corner of necessity-decision scenarios—then we have to start doing our chores and stop giving up our choices. The best way to do that is to take action when it must be taken.

That's our challenge—live by our own choice or be faced with the consequences of a necessity situation we didn't have enough of a hand in designing.

On the next page, you'll find some of the telltale signs of procrastination. Most of us fall prey to at least one of these self-initiated "traps" every day; the trick is to learn to recognize them, so the next time you're tempted to fall into an unproductive pattern of procrastination, you recognize it. Take a moment now to read over the following list, identify any familiar patterns, and remember that all of them, if indulged for too long, lead to necessity (not choice) scenarios.

❀ Bodily procrastination. You've put off taking action on getting that physical, mammogram, or visit to the dentist's office. You tell yourself, "I just can't take the time"—and meanwhile, gingivitis (or worse!) creeps up on you.

❀ Do it right or don't do it at all. Here, "perfectionism" takes the form of paralysis. You wait until you have all of the right tools and have a 100 percent chance of success before you act. That's basically never, so the job doesn't get started.

❀ Sheer frustration. The task you're putting off aggravates and stresses you out, and you figure if there's one thing you don't need, it's more stress. So you take no action.

❀ Fear of failure. This is a biggie. Who wants to fail or look stupid in front of loved ones and peers? Fear convinces many of us not to take action. Unfortunately, *failing* to act often brings us to some scary situations, but we often find ways to overlook this fact, a testament to the power we initially invest in this (illogical) emotional roadblock. This particular procrastination pattern seems to get stronger in later years, and in some extreme cases, can turn into a serious phobia.

❀ Physical discomfort. Sometimes, body parts actually start to ache at the thought of taking action in a given area, and none will admit to liking self-induced pain. For example, thoughts of an upcoming test may upset your stomach or make your chest tighten. That's no fun—better stop thinking about the problem. Meaning you skip studying!

❀ Yes, no, maybe. Indecisiveness, like its second cousin perfectionism, can kill any dream or idea. The temptation here is to wait until every single fact is in, and all of the variables attain 100 percent certainty. Take action? When you haven't taken the third poll, gotten four estimates, and secured five "second opinions"? That wouldn't be prudent! Maybe it makes more sense to see what happens.

These patterns are virtually universal. We all engage in them to some degree. The question is, how do we avoid giving our choices and our lives to someone or something else because of *habitual* entry to procrastination through one of these doors? How do we keep necessity-driven decisions from taking over the show?

Here's a plan of attack you can use to resolve any tendency to procrastinate in areas that will make a big difference in your life. The ideas that follow will help you figure out when it's time to accelerate, rather than procrastinate and show you how to turn on the afterburners. I call it the ACTION plan; it has six steps.

Ascertain

Conclude

Take time

Inventory

Organize

Never look back!

1   Ascertain the seriousness of the procrastination issue. Do you really have a problem here? If you're not certain, ask yourself these five questions. On one or more than one occasion has procrastination created:

    §   A health problem?

    §   A financial consequence?

    §   A personal relationship issue?

    §   A hardship on someone else?

    §   A career setback?

All of the above issues fall into the "zero-tolerance" category. In other words, if you've experienced any of the areas above one single time as a result of a certain pattern of procrastination, that's one time too many! Move on immediately.

2   Conclude what makes you procrastinate. What is it? Frustration? Fear of failure? Fear of the unknown? Perfectionism? Risk? The reason will change according to what's being postponed. Analyze the problem. Write down at least 10 possible reasons you may be putting off action in an area of concern. Then review the list and put check marks by the fear, pain, or loss motivations that seem to be accurate.

Once you've highlighted your negative motivators, put a number alongside each one, and rank them in order of severity. Look at the top three and ask yourself, "If I eliminated these three concerns, would I be able to move forward in this area?" In most cases, your answer will be "Yes!"

For two years, "Daniel" has been saying, "I hate my job. I need to get out and use more of my creative talents!" He wants to begin work in the floral industry. What's standing in the way? Here are Daniel's top negative motivators in order of severity:

- Initially, I'd have to take 20 percent pay cut to start a new career as a florist.

- Although I have a passion for floral design, my skill set is rusty; I may not be able to perform in my new career.

- If it doesn't work out, I'll be *unemployed*! I'll never be able to stand the embarrassment of not having a job!

Daniel's reasons for delay can be transformed into an energizing purpose and direction.

- Daniel should take immediate stock and perform a totally accurate accounting of his daily, weekly, monthly, and yearly expenses. Are there opportunities for cutting back or eliminating expense? Can he save 20 percent by eating out less, relying less on credit cards, and making fewer impulse purchases? If he can, he should put that 20 percent into an interest bearing savings account. In less than six months, he'll be in a more flexible financial position and have less fear about making his career transition.

§ Daniel should start working part-time, evenings or weekends in a local floral shop or take a night school refresher course. If part-time work is hard to find, he should volunteer his time in exchange for on the job training.

§ Daniel should ask his current employer about setting up a six-month leave of absence. Could it hurt to ask? Even if the answer is no, if Daniel sets up a savings plan and increases his skill base, he'll boost his self-esteem and his job market value.

3 Find time to take action. Chip away at your existing behavior and the task about which you've been procrastinating. Take concrete action, even if the task is days or weeks from completion. Let's say it's April 14th and you haven't completed your income tax return, or begun looking through the mountain of receipts on your desk, or found the paperwork you need! It might be impossible to get your taxes filed, but you *could* take and hour to meet with a tax consultant and complete the forms for an extension and schedule a series of follow-up meetings with that person.

Executing this step takes a little self-determination—but you can do it. Examine the dimensions of whatever you've put off. Break it down into small bite-sized pieces. Then pick a certain time each day to do it. It's best to pick the same time of day, a time when you are fresh and alert. Make it your most creative time of day. For some, that's the early morning hours; for others, it's midday. (Interesting side note: In many cultures, a short 20 to 30 minute nap in the middle of the work day provides in essence two "mornings" of fresh and creative energy.) During your peak time, set aside at least 30 or 45 minutes. Make an appointment with yourself. Write it in your daily planner and mark it on your calendar. Then stick to it!

4 Inventory: Take stock of any deficiencies you may have in the questionable area—as well as your strengths. Then take action to minimize the former and maximize and expand the latter. Invest in appropriate self-help or personal development seminars. Read at least one book—or listen to at least one audio program—which offers specific advice in addressing one or more of your problem areas. Start this in the next 30 days and continue it!

5 Organize all resources available to help eliminate the backlog of items and situations you've been procrastinating about. Then get help and take on your challenge! Who in your circle of family, friends, or coworkers can help you get things in order? Once the backlog is eliminated, constantly revisit items 2, 3, and 4 on this list to keep everything in order. (See also item 6.) And remember, you now owe the person or people who helped you out—big time.

6 Never look back! Keep an ongoing to-do list. Create a longer-range plan showing exactly what needs to be done to keep on top of the issues—and then work your plan! Every time you take a step, take a moment to celebrate the accomplishment. Reward yourself in some way for each victory, no matter how small.

These then, are the six steps you can take now to eliminate procrastination in your own life in a given area. The bottom line will always be the same: You must take the time and take action to make a conscious choice, or suffer the consequences that necessity-driven situations present.

Internal and External Events

As I noted at the outset of this chapter, the world offers its share of potentially dismaying events: office politics, world politics, business reversals, large-scale economic shifts, media conniption fits, and so on. Have you ever noticed that some people put things in perspective without getting rattled by the unpredictable developments of the "outside world"?

I believe that the "unrufflability" quotient is a trait we can all learn, but I have to qualify that statement. We each have certain predispositions when it comes to interacting with individuals and situations. We each have certain outlooks and opinions about the people and events in our world. Initially, there are two basic frames of reference—Internal or External—guiding our choices about interactions with people. Whether you are internally or externally oriented towards others, you can learn to relate internally to your situation in a positive way! That means you have control over what situations mean to you—the pleasure or pain you assign to them.

Take a look now at the two major "starting points" when dealing with others.

Internal Frames of Reference

People who have a strong internal frame of reference act as though they've drafted, amended, and ratified a personal Constitution that governs every decision. They have established standards from which they rarely, if ever, deviate. Their "gut feeling," their sense of intuition, plays a prominent role in their daily lives. They may be interested, in an abstract way, in fashion, fads, and others' opinions. They may keep informed about the world around them, but they rarely do or say anything that shows they are interested in *being identified* with the consensus or majority opinion. You may hear these people described as being "in a world all their own."

If someone with a strong internal frame of reference considered making a purchase, and a salesperson said, "So-and-so purchased one of these units and fell in love with it," guess what the response would be? Odds are, that salesperson would hear something like this:

- § Good for her.
- § That's nice!
- § Who cares?
- § I bet that made you happy.

There might be no response at all! People with a strong internal frame of reference have been known to withdraw from conversations that appeal strongly to the values, decisions, or predispositions of others.

External Frames of Reference

People considered to have a strong external frame of reference are concerned with "what's hot" and "what's not." They may reflect mainstream emotions and opinions. They care—often very deeply—about what other people say and do, and their own opinions about the world can be greatly affected by others' opinions. When good gossip makes the rounds, people with strong external frames of reference want all the details. If someone with a strong external frame of reference were about to make a major purchase, and a salesperson said, "So-and-so purchased one of these units the other day and fell in love with it," the response would probably be one that reflected significantly increased interest:

- Really? How do you know he liked it so much?
- What did she like about it?
- Who else has purchased one of these units?
- Could I speak directly with him?

In many situations, when a person with a strong external frame of reference learns that a product is already "selling like hotcakes" or a certain style is in fashion—that's enough information to make the decision. The answer is, "Yes, I want it!"

What's the Best?

Actually, there is no "best" approach—nor is there any right or wrong! Each of these two viewpoints represents an existing predisposition, a particular way of evaluating the world. The trick is to identify and expand on your current style—to try, a little at a time, to broaden your way of interacting with others, so that you get the "best of both worlds."

Strive to benefit from a mix of external and internal reference. Try to consider external influence and opinion, then run those factors through your internal filter. One half of that task will come easily; the other will take practice. Consciously imposing balance in this way will help you learn and will broaden your horizons. Consider the advice my brother, Al, gave me many years ago: "Look at each situation as if it's happening to someone else. Collect the facts, then act as if you're the expert giving advice. Then take it!"

If I had children, I would pass this advice along... but since I don't, I'll share it with you!

Convincing Yourself and Others

There's another "starting point" you should be aware of—the amount of proof necessary to convince someone of something. Perhaps you've had a relationship with someone who needed constant proof of your friendship and constant attention. When that person didn't feel appreciated, the relationship suffered and barriers went up. If you wanted to save the friendship, you had to respond with lots of attention—fast! This was a person who needed significant proof—large amounts of it—to be convinced.

If you've ever connected closely with someone who needed only occasional reinforcement about his or her value as a friend, you were interacting with a person who *didn't* need mountains of proof in key areas. You couldn't *ignore* this person entirely and expect him or her to remain a friend—but you certainly didn't have to provide constant proof.

As with our internal and external references, there is no right or wrong, good or bad style in this area. There's just an existing predisposition.

"This Is a Test!"

When I first moved to California, I packed my 1966 Corvette with my worldly possessions and took Route 66 west until I saw the Pacific Ocean. Then I made a sharp left turn, stopped in San Diego, and looked for employment. I wound up getting a job at an aerospace company in San Marcos, California. My first day on the job, the human resources director asked me if I would like to volunteer "for a test." I looked up and said, "The last time I volunteered for something, I got stuck in a back end of a helicopter for six years." (I guess the Navy had left its lasting impression on me!)

"It's a psychological test," he said. "Well," I thought, "why on earth would they want to know about me? Had they talked to my sister, Phyllis, and learned something unusual about me?" In any event, I respectfully declined the offer. Looking back, I regret this decision—because that HR director was pointing me toward a pioneering test invented by Dr. David Merrill, an industrial psychologist who is now a legend in the field.

As a result of his research and testing, Merrill came up with a world-famous breakdown of personality styles to help people understand and interact in a more effective and meaningful way with the different styles of coworkers, friends, and family.

Although Dr. Merrill's tests were exhaustive and complex, he identified four basic personality categories by means of two observations. The first observation was that people either tend to hold their emotions inside or tend to show their emotions openly and freely; the second was that people, when engaged in conversation, either used a dominant "telling" style or a more reserved, question-driven "asking" style. These two essential continuums led to the four (now-famous) descriptions of personality tendencies as shown on the next page.

You probably have a good idea of the social behavior of these groups by the names Dr. Merrill gave to their styles. Take a closer look at each one now.

These people tend to keep their emotions inside and mostly ask questions when in conversation with others.

The Analytical Style

These people are similar to the Analytical group and tend to keep their emotions inside, but their conversation is more of a telling nature, similar to the Expressive group.

The Driver Style

These people tend to easily show and share their emotions, but are similar to the Analytics in that their conversational style is essentially one of asking.

The Amiable Style

These people tend to show their emotions freely and openly and their conversation has more of a telling style.

The Expressive Style

The Analytical Style

The Analytic loves to deal with facts, figures, and details. These people are deliberate in their actions; you're likely to find them enjoying solitary activities. They tend to prefer a process over interaction with another person or team player. Accuracy and timeliness are their hallmarks. They have a low tolerance for mistakes or misinformation. They can be critical, but they do not like their work criticized by someone they feel to be of lesser authority, capability, or competency. So if you want something done "by the book" and to get as close to the right answer as you can possibly get, give the job to the ultimate problem solver, the Analytic.

Whatever your style, remember that if you want something from the Analytic, never emphasize the possibility (or make the request) that some element of a job may be overlooked or some procedure or checklist ignored. (That may cause hyperventilating on the spot.) Don't encourage this person to "look to the big picture" or "forget about the small stuff." For the Analytic, no detail is too small.

Some of the jobs, assignments, and careers that suit this style are: computer programmer, engineer, CPA/accountant, and project leader. Analytics are usually well organized, even if that organization is not immediately obvious to an outsider. They know where everything is. If you ask an Analytic for a piece of paper, he or she will find it quickly—even though the desk may look like a disaster area. During their time off, Analytics are likely to be engaged in challenging projects that require great ingenuity (such as restoring a classic car or tinkering with a personalized Web page).

Take a moment now to reflect upon the Analytic style—and to find out who, among your family, friends, and coworkers, are the most typical Analytics.

The Expressive Style

The Expressive loves dealing with people and teams. They volunteer to be in the center of any enjoyable and challenging new activity—as long as doing so involves interaction with others. The Expressive loves change and the excitement working with others on new projects can bring. In a group, Expressives are happiest when they're the center of attention. They may be excellent motivators and brainstormers, but they are often not strong on detail or follow-through. They may lose interest quickly, and are usually not comfortable tackling complex, long-term projects or assignments.

Whatever your own personality style, if you need something from an Expressive, highlight the social excitement or "newness" inherent in the situation, and let the other person be the center of attention. Don't demand detailed analysis or reams of compiled data from this person. The Expressive won't deliver—

although he or she would love to hook up with another member of the team who can!

Careers that suit the Expressive may include marketing, sales, public relations, and communications. Typically, organization is not one of the Expressive's strong points. If you ask an Expressive for a document, you're likely to hear something like this: "As soon as it turns up, I'll get it to you." Leisure time may find the Expressive organizing the next block party or volunteering for some cause. These folks are not loners. Night school, associations, gyms—in short (or shorts!), anyplace where there are people gathered is where the Expressive wants to be.

Who in your circle of acquaintances would you identify as an Expressive?

The Driver Style

You'll find the Driver at the helm of the ship. These people love to lead, love being in the "pressure cooker," and love calling the shots. Stress is their middle name; action is their game. They like to make snap decisions and sort problems out later. They tend to be short on close interpersonal relationship building, but are "born politicians" and big on empire building. As you can imagine, careers and job titles that suit the Driver are: any type of leadership position such as entrepreneur, president or CEO, vice president, plant manager, or business owner.

Whatever your own personality style, remember: If you need something from a Driver, be brief, direct, and to the point. Don't challenge this person's authority, in public or in private—unless you're ready for a major conflict. Don't ask questions that force the Driver to admit that he or she doesn't know something; the exchange will stop cold. Focus instead on what the person is trying to accomplish, and make suggestions based on what you hear about that objective.

Drivers usually have tough skins and big egos. If you ask a Driver for a document, he or she is likely to delegate the task to someone else or ask why you really need it. Leisure time—what leisure time? It's hard to tell when a Driver is at rest! These folks are likely involved in some competitive sport or a second career (such as a home-based business) in their "off hours." They may serve on the board of several organizations. At any given moment, they may be reading three or four books at once—none in the fiction category!

Who would you categorize as a Driver in your current relationships?

The Amiable Style

The Amiable is caring, considerate, concerned, and always available for a friend or colleague. These people are great listeners and nurturers. As a general rule, they don't like the limelight. In a meeting, they are likely to wait until it's over, then track down a colleague and say, "I didn't want to bother you or interrupt the meeting, but I'd like to make a suggestion, if I could... " They are extremely dependable and supportive.

Whatever your own personality style, remember: If you want something from an Amiable, emphasize how important your ongoing relationship is or what contribution they can make—and always act in a way that supports and respects that relationship. Don't ask this person to "choose sides" or "stand up and be counted" in an organizational dispute if you can possibly avoid it. You should also avoid deadlines and ultimatums when dealing with this person; Amiables don't like high-pressure situations, but would never tell you that!

Loyalty comes with the territory for an Amiable. Suitable careers and positions are customer service and support, administrative positions, human resources, and counselor. They are wonderful listeners; they want to help anyone and everyone. On days off, the Amiable is nesting. Single, married, or parent—it doesn't matter. Amiables nest. They are helpful in the neighborhood. If there is a need, they want to fill it. If someone on the block is sick or in a difficult family situation, they'll offer help.

Who are the Amiables in your life?

What's Your Style?

Do the four styles we've examined sound familiar? Did one seem appropriate to your own style?

We each have a primary style and a secondary style. We operate out of our primary style most of the time and, on occasion, we show traits of our secondary style. What's probably most important for you now is to confirm your primary style while developing a sense of what will and won't work when you're trying to interact with someone of a different or similar style.

In an organization, family, or other group, harmonious outcomes will be most likely to arise when each member focuses on his or her "strong suit"—and nobody challenges his or her right or ability to do so. Consider the following brief story:

Driver, Analytic, Expressive and Amiable are in the same family and are planning their summer vacation to Wonder World, the nation's biggest theme park. Although it's only January, Analytic has developed a comprehensive breakdown and perhaps a diagram of how bags will be packed. It's all on a checklist: clothing, camera gear, first-aid kit, maps, and walking tour instructions are identified so that everyone will be ready to go. Expressive is working on a press release to e-mail to all interested parties about their plans, with agenda attached listing phone numbers where they can be reached. Driver is trying to talk the Analytic, Expressive, and Amiable into flying on the "red-eye" Friday night and returning on the earliest flight Thursday so she doesn't miss too many workdays. Amiable is quietly working behind the scenes, making sure special meals are ordered on every flight, and ensuring that the hotel will have a non-smoking room blocked out, as per plan.

Now it's time to confirm what your own primary style is. Get a piece of paper and reproduce the simple chart shown on the next page.

Now answer the following questions without placing any preconditions. (Stay away from formulations like, "It depends on..." or "only if..." or "only when..." Stick with strong initial responses.)

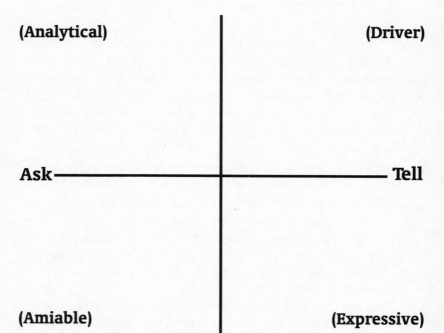

1 Do you tend to keep your emotions inside? If so, place an "x" on the line that leads to "Hold Inside." If it's hard for others to tell when you're excited or how you feel about a certain issue, chances are you keep emotions inside. The more you repress emotions, the higher your "x" should be placed on that line toward "Hold Inside."

2 Do you tend to openly show your emotions? If you use lots of body language when you communicate and your facial expressions are highly animated, chances are you're comfortable with showing your emotions. If this is the case, place an "x" close to the line that leads to "Openly Show."

The more you display your emotions, the lower your "x" should be placed on that line toward "Openly Show."

Note: You should only select one of these first two choices. You either hold emotions inside or you openly show them.

3   In conversations, do you tend to have more of a "telling" (or "controlling") style? I don't mean talkative—I mean controlling, if not dominating. If so, place an "x" close to the line that leads to "Tell." The greater your tendency to control a conversation, the closer your "x" should be placed on that line toward "Tell."

4   In conversations, do you tend to have more of an "asking" (or "conforming") style? If you can't remember the last time you interrupted someone, or rarely interrupt other people, you should answer "Yes" to this question. If you do, place an "x" close to the line that leads to "Ask." The more you tend to conform in a conversation, the closer your "x" should be placed on that line toward "Ask."

Note: Here again, you'll either pick number three or four to be true.

Remember: There is no right or wrong communication style!

The world of is made up of different styles (and different combinations of primary and secondary styles). Don't be concerned if your style doesn't match the sample careers I've listed; these are just indications from my own personal observations of what careers are best-suited to various styles.

Add Style to Your Chart!

Now that you've got your two "x"s on your chart, fill in the styles shown on the next page.

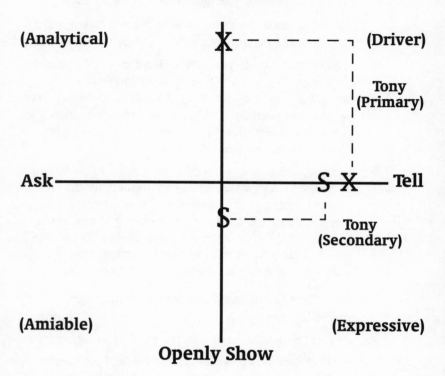

What's Your Secondary Style?

Did you feel as though you *occasionally* show some characteristics discussed previously—but didn't do so often enough to justify a particular answer? If so, take the test again, and give your secondary traits free rein. Just so you can keep your primary and secondary style separated put a small "s" instead of the "x" on the line in the appropriate spots. Answer the questions again—however, now you should feel free to say to yourself: "It depends on..." or "only if..." or "only when..."

Get a Second Opinion!

You should now have someone you know well on a social basis answer the four "style" questions with you in mind. Repeat this process with someone at work, who you don't consider a close friend. (Warning: This will be hard to do if you're an Expressive—but do it anyway.)

Pay special attention to the styles chosen by your close relationships and your workplace peers. If they come up with the same answers and choose the same style, your self-image is identical to the image you project. Take a moment and think about some of your family members, peers at work, and your friends. Can you identify each primary style? Does the style you select fit well with their everyday behavior and your own memory of their interactions with you and others?

Interacting with the Different Styles

Have you ever experienced a situation where you walked away from a conversation thinking "What's wrong with him?" or "Who put a bug in her bonnet?" Usually nothing is wrong; it's just that you didn't consider the right approach necessary to communicate effectively with that person's style. Perhaps, without realizing it, you asked an Amiable to "stand up and be counted" in a way that intimidated this consensus-driven person. Or perhaps you posed a series of technical questions that left a Driver feeling as though you'd launched an attack against his or her authority because he or she didn't have the answers or was unfamiliar with the topic.

I've already offered you some initial ideas on communicating with people of various styles—basic strategies that will help you get what you want without stepping on people's toes. You should also know that certain styles mix well, while others clash.

So, beyond targeting your appeals effectively by respecting a person's innate style, you should also consider what kinds of working relationships are likely to prosper (or not prosper) over an extended period. In most cases, this process has little or nothing to do with personal failings or talent mismatches; the primary personality styles involved lead to a scenario where people "rub each other the wrong way."

Keep these rules in mind whenever you select your team or figure out who should tackle what with whom in a family setting.

1   "Like" styles do not necessarily get along or work well together.

2   Styles that are situated on our chart directly "across" or "perpendicular" from each other generally have a more difficult time working together.

3   Styles that are "up and down" from each other are more likely to interact harmoniously.

By remaining sensitive to the other person's communication style, and by teaming up with people who are likely to interact effectively with you, you'll greatly increase the likelihood that your interactions with others will be constructive and harmonious.

Take Action—and Point Yourself in the Right Direction!

Los Angeles, Summer 1969. There I was, barreling down the highway with a friend, smiling from ear to ear behind the wheel of my '66 Corvette. We had the top down. We had the music blasting. We were exceeding the speed limit. Life was perfect.

Suddenly, my companion noticed a sign hurtling by. A look of concern came over her face; she said something, but with all the delicious wind, I couldn't hear what she said. I shrugged my shoulders and put a hand to my ear. Then my friend yelled at the top of her lungs: "We're lost! You're going in the wrong direction!"

I said, "Who cares? We're making great time!"

In some respects I haven't changed much over the years. I have a little less hair (okay, a lot less hair), I still drive too fast, and I still get lost from time to time. But what has changed for me is that today I understand myself and others, and that means I usually have a pretty clear sense of where I am, where I need to be going, and how I can get there. Oh, don't get me wrong. I still get confused. You see, I don't always head in the right direction or understand others in exactly the way I should. But I don't waste any more time being lost than I possibly have to. Why? The pressure's on! I have less time to waste than I did back in '69! Who has enough time to high-tail it to nowhere? Not me! (The truth is, I never had enough time for that. I just didn't know it at the time!)

You're reading this book because you want to get to some destination while you still have the health, time, and money to enjoy your arrival at that destination. Before you pull out of the driveway, take the time to understand yourself and others around you. Find out what really makes you tick. Make sure you know which way the "vehicle" you're driving is best pointed. Then put the top down, turn the volume up and hit the gas! Yeah—life is perfect!

～ Chapter 4 ～

Getting Passionate about the Right Goals

I believe that when you truly put your whole self into achieving a goal, without reservation, you're bound to succeed. In this chapter, you'll learn how to connect those goals to your personal style of perceiving and learning and you'll discover how your unique values, beliefs, and qualities influence that process. You'll learn to get in touch (or back in touch) with your sense of purpose, and how to take full responsibility for truly living your life's plan.

Your Passion

Let's talk about passion—the necessary foundation of achieving any worthwhile goal.

Passion is an intense emotion or powerful enthusiasm for a person or cause. I hope you'll agree that any goal which doesn't inspire passion is a goal that probably needs fine-tuning... or must be drastically changed!

In the last chapter, we found that of the four major personality styles, the Analytic and the Driver had a tendency to hold emotions inside. But the Amiable and Expressive had a tendency to show their emotions more easily. This doesn't mean only those two personality groups ever show passion!

Don't mistake "emotion" for "passion"! Whether or not they lay all their cards on the table, Drivers can get enthusiastic about their mission, and Analytics can show remarkable intensity for objectives they're pursuing.

No, the key here is to not think about personality types but about the way we process various information. That's what helps us connect passion to our goals and make effective appeals to the goals of others.

So, how do people decide to be passionate about something?

See It, Hear It, Feel It

Have you ever been in a situation where someone frustrated you by "ignoring" the obvious that you saw with your own two eyes?

Have you ever talked to someone until nearly blue in the face—and been unable to get the person to connect with what you were trying to say?

Have you ever tried to show someone something simple through a first-hand "here's how you do it" demonstration but only succeeded in getting a blank stare or asked where to find the manual?

If you've experienced anything like the above frustrations, rest assured you're not alone. Researchers Richard Bandler and John Grinder (a psychologist and mathematician, respectively) found that expressions and judgments fell into three major categories, despite personal temperament or personality type.

Bandler and Grinder found that people followed one of three major patterns when it came to making internal and external judgments and understanding new situations:

❀ Visual ("Seeing is believing.")

❀ Auditory ("Just tell me the facts.")

❀ Kinesthetic ("I've got the feel of it now.")

Most frustrating "crossed-wires" exchanges arise because we're trying to pass along information in a way that we favor— but that really is not easily accessible to the other person. Let's look at each of the three groups in more detail.

Visual Learners

If you're a member of this group, you see things clearly in your mind, with little effort. When you read text or listen to someone, you automatically "draw mental pictures." You visualize scenes naturally.

For the record, I'm a visual learner; I can "see" all of the villages I visited as I walked more than 350 miles through the Himalayas. Right now, with only the slightest conscious effort, I can vividly recall the faces of the Sherpas who helped carry my gear.

Is being able to recall those things a big advantage for me? Well, sure, sometimes. But keep in mind that I have a more difficult time recalling village names—or the people's! I'm much better with faces than names—a classic preference of visual learners.

Visual learners have certain easy-to-identify habits. They frequently use words that key into their preference for visual sights. They really will say things like:

𝄞 Do you get the picture?

𝄞 Can't you just see it?

𝄞 What's your point of view on this?

𝄞 Why don't you just show me?

𝄞 Imagine this...

𝄞 That's brilliant!

People who are visually oriented tend to look at you a certain way. Have you ever noticed how some people gaze at you with a blank stare when you speak—as though they look through you?

When that happened, the odds are you were talking to a visual learner who envisioned what you were saying as you said it.

Communicating with a person who has a strong visual preference can be fun, because you can almost tell what's going on in this person's mind by watching his or her eyes. Hard to believe, but it's true. If I ask a person with a visual learning preference about something pertaining to the future, that person will usually look up and to the right.

Let's say I'm talking to Roxanne, a friend of mine, and she's a visual learner. I say, "Roxanne, do you think you'll be able to help me work on the floor plan for my mountain cabin next Wednesday night?"

If Roxanne looks up and to the right, she is most likely "seeing" her next week's calendar in her mind.

As a general rule, when visual learners look up to the *left*, there's a good chance that they're preoccupied with something in the past. So, if Roxanne looks up and to the left when I ask that same question, she may be thinking about what happened the last time she helped me with something.

If Roxanne stares straight ahead at me, with an almost unfocused look, she may be undecided. Perhaps she's trying to internalize your request somehow—and visualize the outcome. If you find yourself dealing with a visual learner who stares off into the distance, you may be able to win the person over by emphasizing visual elements in your vocabulary and speech.

"Come on—you always come up with such brilliant ideas, we'll be able to finish in a flash, and then I'll show you that new shop in the mall. Can you see any way to make the time?"

(The words "brilliant," "flash," "show," and "see" are likely to have more impact on this person than on people in the other two categories.)

Remember, if you want a visual person to "catch your wave," and understand your dream or passion, you must make sure the person can "see" what's on your mind. If they can't see it, they won't believe it!

Auditory Learners

The auditory person prefers sound above just about any other form of sensory and communication input. The way you deliver your message will be critical to getting this person on your side. People who talk a lot about "hearing things out," or constantly ask you to "listen" to what they're saying, may be auditory learners. People who want to "talk through" problems, and who seem to make decisions through discourse and conversation, are likely to be auditory learners.

Does the person you're talking to prefer listening to audio-tapes (whether or not while driving) rather than reading? Is this person likely to ask you to "summarize" a memo or report, rather than read it? If so, you're likely interacting with an auditory learner.

Suppose Roxanne is an auditory learner and you want to win her help or support for something. To begin, use highly descriptive words, and recognize that word selection alone won't win the person over. Your tone of voice, the pitch, and speech rate will all play important roles in establishing this person's belief.

The most common mistake people make in dealing with auditory learners is to raise the volume when they're trying to make a point or add excitement to a message. To someone sensitive to sound, this is usually an instant turnoff. It's much better to raise the *pitch* of your voice when you want to show emotion or excitement.

Never use a droning "monotone" voice when speaking to an auditory learner. (This is a bad idea when you're interacting with a visual or kinesthetic learner, but it's the kiss of death when interacting with someone using speech and hearing as the primary channel for communication.)

Always modulate your voice and be careful to avoid the equally irritating "sing-song" style that incorporates only two or three vocal "notes." Pause—for a good two seconds or longer—when making an important point.

Note: To reach full mastery in gaining the support and belief of the auditory learner, you may want to join the local chapter of Toastmasters. This organization teaches effective communication skills for dealing with the auditory learner.

Kinesthetic Learners

These people are likely to believe or support you only if they "get a feeling about" your message. They're "touchy-feely" people who prefer direct interaction with people and things. You'll be able to pick them out almost instantly, because their handshakes tend to last noticeably longer than those of visual or auditory learners—they really do like to touch.

Many kinesthetic learners will touch your forearm with their left hand while shaking hands. They're driven by feelings and emotions, and will sometimes back away from making key decisions because they "don't feel good" about them. Kinesthetic learners are also fond of taking cars (and ideas!) "out for a test drive" and getting "hands-on experience."

These people put a premium on emotional connection—feelings and person-to-person contact count for quite a bit. They like to connect on a "gut" level. Your challenge is to find a way to help this person connect with your plan, dream, or objective on a visceral level.

So, if Roxanne is a kinesthetic learner, and you want her support or help, you should get close (be appropriate, not threatening), use eye contact, and perhaps touch her shoulder or forearm briefly before speaking about emotional bonding, shared experience, and one-on-one attention.

It could sound like this:

"Roxanne, I feel that you're the very best person to help me get a handle on the plans for my mountain cabin. Could we touch base on Wednesday night for a couple of hours—or do you have another idea? Oh, by the way, afterward, we could go to a new outdoor store I found at the mall, one I really think you'd love. It will be a great experience!"

To appeal to a kinesthetic learner, emphasize words like "feel," "handle," "touch base," "love," and "experience."

Why do I share all of this with you? Because knowing how a person processes information is essential to excite someone about your goals. But guess what? Knowing how *you* process information is essential to excite *yourself* about your *own* goals! In other words, you need to "target" key messages about your goals to yourself, not just to others.

Success Messages

This was a breakthrough discovery for me, and I think there's a good chance it can also lead you to a breakthrough. Let me explain how I made this discovery.

Several years ago, I gave a speech to over 100 executives at a leading telecommunications company. I had just finished the portion of my program where I discussed visual, auditory, and kinesthetic ways of communicating. As part of this discussion, I illustrated the differences between the three patterns, and had the members of the audience "place" themselves in their own predominant mode. (To do this, they used a condensed self-diagnostic exercise similar to the one I'm about to pass along to you.) I did a quick headcount in each group.

Then I moved on to my next topic, goal-setting. I asked the group a question.

"All right, before we get started, how many people here have taken the time to write down their current goals?"

Only visual learners raised their hands. I knew they were the same people who'd identified themselves as visual, because I'd just counted that group. Now, this was a group of over 100 senior managers, each with a four-year degree and somewhere between five and fifteen years of management experience. I knew these people had been told repeatedly over the years about the importance of formalizing goals in writing, but the only people who'd responded to that message—at least about their current goals—were operating within the visual learning style.

Maybe, I thought to myself, people should communicate about their own goals in a way that respects their primary style.

Once that thought flashed across my brain, I was speechless, which is a rare event for an Italian public speaker. But I realized it was true. If you want results, if you want to grow, if you want to achieve your full potential, then you must start by sending a clear message to your brain—a message your brain will understand, process, and, most importantly, believe.

Perhaps, by reading this far, you've already got a strong sense of your favorite communication style. Still, I encourage you to do the following exercise to establish, with a high degree of accuracy, whether you process information in a visual, auditory, or kinesthetic way.

This is a fun exercise—one you can do with a spouse, companion, close friend, or a peer at work. Obtain a small notebook. Start the exercise on a weekday. For the next 24 hours, take three or four minutes to post journal entries on what you see, hear, and feel on the following occasions:

- § When you first wake up
- § Before you begin work or start your daily routine
- § Before you eat lunch
- § Before you eat dinner
- § Before you get into bed and call it a day

At each of the above points, write at least three observations in each category: seeing, hearing, and feeling. (The best way to successfully complete this exercise is to use separate sheets of paper for each activity at each point in the day. You'll have a separate sheet for noting what you *see* when you wake up, another sheet for what you *hear* when you wake up, and so on.)

At the end of 24 hours, give your notebook to the other person and ask for help in determining your preference.

Does what you wrote focus most intently on the pictures you saw (visual learning), the sounds you heard (auditory learning),

or your feelings (kinesthetic learning)? Your partner will probably notice a trend or strong tendency toward one of these three
options. The closest runner-up is your secondary communication mode.

Please, put this book down for a day and return to it only
after you've completed the notebook exercise!

Now That You Know

Welcome back. You now have a good idea of your favorite communication style. This information will be valuable as you move
toward goals that make sense for you.

People internalize their goals in different ways. I've already
pointed out my strong visual preference. In order for a visual
learner (like me) to speak to his or her brain in a way that *the
brain* clearly understands, that person will have to "see" the positive (not the negative!) consequences of working toward goals.

Why? Because visual judgments are our first instinct. We
need to draw a picture and register the positive consequences.
You may not be a visual learner, though. If you're an auditory
person, you'll need to hear about your goals. If you're kinesthetic, you'll need to learn how to feel your goals emotionally
through physical relaxation.

Later in this chapter, I'll show you how to generate a complete list of what you find rewarding in your life, and how to
fine-tune the rewards you seek. For now, I'm assuming that
you've already got something you're eager to accomplish, so I
can illustrate the importance of selecting the correct medium
for your own primary communication style. Then you can send
"success messages" to your brain in the most appealing way.

If You're a Visual Learner...

...you'll want to learn goal-mapping. To use this technique, you
must be willing to draw pictures. The pictures don't have to be
perfect. What's important is that they be yours.

Go back to the work you did in Chapter One; pick out a favorite belief bridge. Select a belief that supports a goal or dream

you want to accomplish. (For instance, if you want to land a new job that pays significantly more than you're currently earning, you'll want to select a belief that furthers this goal. Perhaps, "I add value to every situation I encounter.")

Now, draw a picture of your life, and/or a situation the way it is today, on the left side of your bridge. Use as many descriptive icons and illustrations as you can. For ideas, look at my own goals map (below).

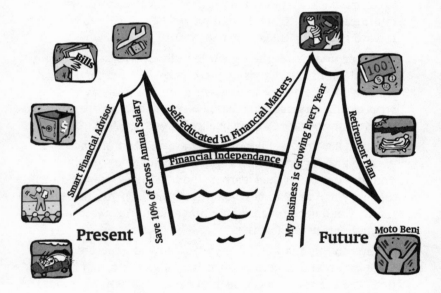

Next, draw a picture on the *right* side of the bridge that illustrates the way your life will be *after* you realize the goal or dream your belief supports. Take a look at my map.

Once you've completed both drawings, find a way to regularly expose yourself to this visual stimulus. I suggest that you take this goals map and tape it to your bathroom mirror. Or laminate it and hang it in your shower. Or reduce the size and carry it in your wallet. Or place it on your dashboard, prop it up next to your computer screen, or create a screen saver with it! Look at it frequently—internalize it. Your mind will gain greater strength to make your goal a reality.

If You're an Auditory Learner...

...listen to prerecorded self-improvement audiotapes—and then make your own!

You may already have a self-help program that appeals to you, and you should be ready to use it. But remember, of all the people you know and listen to, your mind should pay attention to *you* the most. You are the master; the mind is your servant! The spoken word is how your mind processes information, so make a point of using audiotapes to internalize your goals. Program yourself for success.

If you don't have one, purchase or borrow a small tape recorder. Script your life's goals and dreams in story form or write a detailed explanation about the benefits you'll enjoy as a result of achieving your goal. How will meeting this goal improve you personally, professionally, financially, and physically? Don't leave anything or anyone out, and be sure to record everything you say *as though your success is taking place in the present moment*. Here's an example of what I would say as an auditory learner creating a tape that pointed me toward the achievement of an important goal:

> ❁ I am becoming even more successful as I use one of my greatest gifts—my gift of being a special, compassionate person placed on earth to help others. I am living my dream by taking this gift and creating a book about putting the Power of Will to full use. Friends and relatives are reading this book along with thousands of people I've never met. They are delighted by what they are reading, and are supporting me with beaming smiles, words of appreciation, and letters of thanks...

See how it works? Incorporate as many details as possible. Focus on people's facial expressions, the pleasurable actions you and others take, and the rewards and appreciation you receive.

Write a script that hits all the key points—then recite your success into the tape recorder.

Your audiotape should be no longer than 10 minutes in length, and the entire tape should probably include pleasant background music at the beginning and end—or perhaps as you talk. Just be sure that the music you use is something *other* than your favorite tune. The music should be a supporting element, pleasant but neutral—it should not distract or remind you of particular places, times, and experiences.

Take this tape everywhere, and listen to it when you can: during your morning commute, or if you work at home or in a virtual office, before you start your work day. As an aside, if you work at home you can still commute to work. Walk out of your home and walk back in! If you need quiet time, make your stroll a bit longer. While walking, driving, or heading to the gym for a workout, you might choose to alternate your tape with tapes from a favorite motivational speaker. The result: Your mind will get the food and nutrition it needs to apply strength and power to attaining your goals.

If You're a Kinesthetic Learner...

...emphasize the emotional connections with your goal by meditating.

As a kinesthetic learner, you are influenced by emotional states linked to particular physical sensations—by gut-level feelings. If a goal doesn't feel right, you will have difficulty internalizing it and putting the full force of your mind behind it. Meditating on a regular basis is probably the best way to turn future goals and dreams into reality.

Most kinesthetic learners find it fairly easy to meditate. There are many different techniques. The simplest and most effective is to find a quiet place where you won't be disturbed, and to respond to mental distractions by returning to a simple activity: paying attention to your own inner thoughts, or perhaps repeating a mantra.

A mantra is a word or short phrase you repeat mentally. It can be a sentence from a favorite holy text, a positive thought or phrase (love, power, victory, full abundance), or even a nonsense word. The mantra's purpose is to focus and calm your mind. Many runners have learned to repeat mantras such as: lift your knees or stay on pace. If you run, and channel that one phrase through your mind over and over again, there will be no room for debate about what your body should be doing.

I usually advise kinesthetic learners to develop a mantra to stop the natural scattershot thought process most of us experience. Once the mind is quiet, use a meditative monologue to experience emotions connected with the attainment of future goals and dreams.

Here's how it works. First, select a mantra that makes you feel good—I like the word "harmony"—and sit quietly in a private place, repeating the word silently over and over again. (No, you don't have to cross your legs or stand on your head—simply pick out a comfortable chair and repeat the phrase mentally.)

Don't fight distracting thoughts or criticize yourself for having them. Simply put them down and return to your mantra when you realize you're thinking about something else.

After five or ten minutes, your mind will feel still and calm—you'll be in the zone. (If you're totally bored or preoccupied with other thoughts, give it up and try another time, another day.) Now use your meditative monologue. This dialogue should focus on emotions you will feel after reaching a key goal you've selected. It might sound something like this.

> ✿ I feel joy as words flow from my heart and soul, through my fingers, and onto my computer screen. The words I write shimmer and glow; they bring love, happiness, and peace to everyone who comes in contact with them. The words I write make me feel energized, focused, powerful, and happy. I feel as if I can write for hours and the words will flow. In the end, I will have my newest book, *The Power of Will*, completed.

Give your meditation period at least 15 minutes a day—and give it the *right* 15 minutes. The best times to meditate for a positive impact are immediately upon awakening and just before you go to sleep.

There are other ways to feel your goals. Let's imagine your dream is to finish college, and you are three years from achieving that goal. But you're demoralized about it. You find it difficult to juggle a full-time job while raising a family and attending night classes. Emotionally, your dream seems to be fading.

What to do? Attend the next scheduled graduation exercises! Congratulate and talk to as many alumni as you can. Talk to employed individuals who have the same degree that you're working toward. The (temporary) emotional boost you receive will reinspire and reenergize your self-determination.

Passion and Purpose

So now you know how to talk to yourself about your goals—but what should your goals *be*? You may have a sense of what you want to accomplish from the exercises you performed in the spirituality chapter, but now it's time to get a clear fix on what you want and why you want it.

A good goal, one worth reinforcing via the methods we've just examined, should arouse your passion—and support your purpose for living.

How do you find a goal that does both things? How do you discover a dream worth turning into a reality? Here's one strategy that will help.

Earlier in the book, I asked you to develop a list of gifts as part of your Personal Value Inventory. Pull out your inventory list and copy your gifts into the center of the chart on the next page. (If you want, you can make a chart of your own, so that you can edit and expand on things a little more easily.)

Now ask yourself the following questions. Don't skip any question or leave any element blank.

Make Me Smile!   **Intellectually Rewarding**

My Unique Gifts

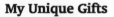

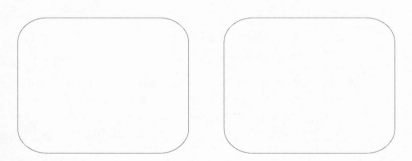

Emotionally Rewarding   **Financially Rewarding**

❀ What activity do you perform on an hourly, weekly, monthly, or yearly basis that makes you really happy? What activities put a big smile on your face? Identify at least one activity (but several would be much better)—make sure it *always* leaves you feeling great. Write this activity down, or draw a picture of it, in the upper left corner.

✿ What activity do you perform on an hourly, weekly, monthly, or yearly basis that rewards you intellectually? Think of an activity that uses mind power, and may leave you feeling intellectually exhausted, but somehow refreshed. Write this activity, or draw a picture of it, in the upper right corner.

✿ What activity do you perform on an hourly, daily, weekly, monthly, or yearly basis that is emotionally rewarding? Think of an activity that leaves you feeling exhilarated and excited. What activity carries the biggest emotional pay-off? Write this activity, or draw a picture of it, in the lower left corner.

✿ What activity do you perform on an hourly, daily, weekly, monthly, or yearly basis that provides significant short-term financial rewards? We're talking about the base hits in your financial world—the bonus you take to the bank. Write this or draw a picture of it in the lower right corner. This could be as simple as paying down your credit card bills, putting 10 percent into a 401(K), or joining a savings club.

Once you've completed this exercise, continue with the following analysis questions:

✿ Are any rewarding activities repeated in more than one category? (This may signal that you should focus more energy on that activity—if the same activity makes you happy and helps you secure short-term financial gain, it should be getting lots of your time.)

✿ How do your rewarding activities match your gifts? (One of my gifts is my sense of humor. That gift connects with my writing and speaking activities, which are emotionally and fiscally rewarding.

If every one of your unique gifts matches up with one of your rewarding activities, then you've got a good basic set of matchups—and are well-positioned to focus more time and attention on rewarding activities. Your success will be almost guaranteed.

If there are few connections, then discover ways that your gifts can be enhanced or improved to make the connections—so each one can be related to at least one of your rewarding activities.

If there are *no* connections, there's a problem. Either you've got a disabling gift—one that's preventing you from taking part in your most rewarding activities—or you need to review your rewarding activities list for accuracy. An example of the first situation—the gift that stands in the way of activities you enjoy—would be a gift for analysis that translates into a tendency to lecture or criticize without giving others a chance to respond. If you've identified connecting emotionally with family as one of the things that gives you greatest emotional pleasure, but find that you intimidate or alienate family members with criticisms, your "gift" is actually a disabling one and needs to be improved.

People taking full advantage of the Power of Will constantly search for ways to make self-improvements that enhance their gifts—so that each one can be related to at least one of their rewarding activities.

When all of your gifts match up with all the activities that are the most rewarding in life, and when you are acting in accordance with your own best and deepest values and beliefs, then you will live with a guiding sense of purpose: The Power of Will.

Once you've identified something you want to change in the above equation—a pattern of behavior blocking an activity you love, or a gift that needs some fine-tuning and self-improvement—how do you make that change? How do you shift negative behavior patterns that have the force of old habits to work in your favor?

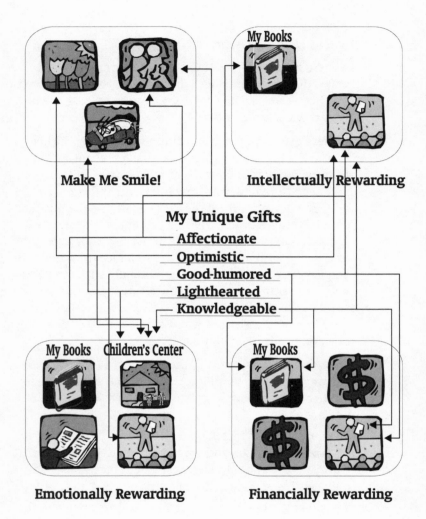

The Finished Product

Because I am a visual learner, I took the time to connect my "matches." Now, it's easy for me to see how supportive my gifts are to my most rewarding actuvities.

Changing Outlooks, Changing Outcomes

- ♪ "I'm on a roll."
- ♪ "I was in the zone."
- ♪ "Nothing succeeds like success."

~

- ♪ "I hit a slump."
- ♪ "I was in the doldrums."
- ♪ "We were riding out a losing streak."

I think we've all heard sayings like these, and understood, on an intuitive level, the experiences they describe. Success really can breed success—and failure really can lead to future failure. But why?

There is a fairly simple answer to that question. Our brains set up different templates based on information from our past history. Our brains constantly associate our current experiences with past experiences. When we encounter stimuli that evoke slump, our brains go into a slump state—and we may stay there for a while. When we encounter stimuli that get us in the zone, our brains go into the zone state—and we may stay there for a while, too. (Remember how that whiff of vanilla-flavored coffee instantly transported me to an incredibly positive frame of mind?)

This process often leads to the pronounced ups and downs we associate with winning and losing streaks. Our brains fill in the blanks by distorting the situation in a dramatic way, meaning that our performance and outlook can shift up or down, depending on what we expect from a situation.

When it comes to making a change, taking a risk, or facing the unknown, our brains have opportunities to fill in the blanks. If our brains fill in every blank positively, that's great! But it will only access this positive information from memory—or from new information you feed it. (Remember, our brains can't tell the difference between real and imagined situations!)

It's very important to remember that the brain can go into slump mode without our even realizing it. We have to make a conscious effort to take control. Let me illustrate what I'm talking about.

Recently, Jeff was almost late for a flight. While running through the airport, he experienced extreme shortness of breath. He barely caught the plane, and he wasn't too happy about the tightness around his chest. He decided that, once he got home, he would see his doctor for that long overdue physical.

The doctor told Jeff that he had to lose weight and eliminate most fats from his diet—which meant no more hot dogs and beer at the baseball games he loved to attend. Jeff's instant initial response to this news sent the following message to his brain:

- No more beer. No more hot dogs. Saturdays will never be the same. I might as well give up my season tickets! I'll never be able to pull this diet off—he wants me to stop eating everything that tastes good. Well, I'll give it a try, but I make no guarantees.

Jeff's brain knows what this message means—Jeff feels cheated, deprived, and let down by the "choice" he had to make. This response was based on his past negative experiences with diets—and, unless Jeff makes a conscious effort to shift his reaction to his situation, he's simply going to continue the negative chain reaction. Jeff allowed his brain to fill in the blanks with negative defaults—and he's geared for defeat. Instead, he might choose to fill in those blanks with positive defaults.

- The doctor says that if I can make a change in what I eat, I'll dramatically increase my chances of making it to age 70. So I guess I've got a choice—eating the occasional hot dog, or seeing my granddaughter graduate from college 15 years from now. What a great experience that will be! And if I can lose a few pounds, I bet my energy level would go up, too, which would probably mean I could get more done at work and spend more time traveling with my wife. You know what? This is going to work out fine.

Positive Change and Realizing Your Passion

To live with greater passion, as someone who takes advantage of the Power of Will, you have to embrace the idea of change.

If you're not quite certain about what needs changing in your life, that's okay. What's important is that you learn to accept the change *process*. Most people are inherently averse to change. Past experiences may have convinced us that change is risky and filled with uncertain outcomes. That is true, but change is the only avenue available to those who wish to grow.

The people who get the most out of life are those who *change what doesn't work and replace it with something that does work*. As a trainer and success counselor, I've found that people who can take full advantage of this principle assume a certain, distinctive mindset—one based on a set of values, qualities, traits, and gifts that *support*, rather than *frustrate* change.

To encourage positive change and realize your passion, you must, at a bare minimum, be willing to:

- Embrace *qualities* like courage and self-determination.
- Encourage *traits* like discipline and the ability to keep everything in perspective.
- Nurture *gifts* like being kind, considerate and helpful toward others.

To be a change master, you must be willing to develop a strong constitution and totally commit yourself to your own values. You need to reinforce a response to adversity by saying "I can" (not "This diet stuff never works for me," or, "I make no guarantees," or, "Maybe it will work, and maybe it won't"). You must choose internal language that supports your belief and puts the Power of Will to work.

Over the years, I've worked with a lot of people who developed a commitment to positive change. Here are the traits they share:

- *They're accountable.* They live by a code. "If it's to be, it's up to me."

❁ *They're confident.* They have a strong belief and faith in themselves, and they constantly reinforce that belief.

❁ *They want to find out more.* They're in constant "search mode"—they want to find ways to improve themselves and develop their strengths.

❁ *They're generous.* They're always trying to find ways to help others grow and develop.

❁ *They embrace new situations and new challenges.* They look at change as an opportunity to benefit by using each of the above strengths, making them even stronger.

Change Has a Pattern!

How do you learn to embrace change when it's not your first or your strongest instinct? You learn to sense the patterns change may take. Here's how change masters do it, time and time again. They use a five-step process that you, too, can use to accept every single change you may face in pursuit of your passion.

❁ *Step one: Be prepared.* Benefit from your own past experience. Look for positive situations that arose from similar past changes. Focus on what actually worked, how you actually grew, and what you actually gained by changing in a similar situation. Don't send negative messages! (If you're trying to take control of your household spending, you might summon up five examples of when you took control in your life and benefited as a result—maybe the time you quit smoking.)

❁ *Step two: Know your options.* Explore all the avenues. Learn everything you can about the situation you face. Find an expert, hit the library, or scan cyberspace—but do something to expand your knowledge base about the area in which you face change. For example, you want to change your personal retirement strategy and portfolio. (If you do this, you'll find that many experts suggest that you track and understand your own personal household expenses *before* implementing any sophisticated retirement or financial plan.)

❀ *Step three: Exercise one option at a time.* An engineer troubleshooting a faulty machine replaces one piece at a time in order to avoid overcorrecting. Similarly, you should try one and only one of your options at a time. (Perhaps monitor each purchase over a one-month period so you can fully quantify your exact discretionary income. Then you can...)

❀ *Step four: Measure your result.* What impact have your actions had? Are you moving in the right direction? (For instance, if you're trying to change your financial pattern, you might monitor your expenses, and then, after 30 days, assign each monthly expense one of three colors: green for essentials like groceries and shelter; yellow for elective expenses like books, magazines, entertainment, and nights out; and red for "what was I thinking" expenses, like Home Shopping Network sprees or the third pair of shoes of the month.)

❀ *Step five: Act on that result.* If the result is good, try to make it better or repeat it as necessary. If the result falls short, go back to step two and explore another option. (Can you eliminate some items that fall into the yellow category—and *all* of the items in the red category? Can you keep up this monitoring exercise on a month-by-month basis?)

This continuous five-step process is a recipe for ongoing positive change that people who utilize the Power of Will build into their lives until it becomes second nature.

Stop Keeping Score

I love helping other people out and giving them things. The problem is that occasionally (all right, frequently), I keep score. I make a mental "you-owe-me-one" note.

Just the other day, I held the door open for a young mother who had a small baby in her arms and a one-year-old in tow. She didn't even give me a smile, let alone a verbal "Thank you." I thought to myself, "There go two kids who will grow up to be selfish," which is funny because, at that moment, I was the one being selfish! By holding that thought, I had completely undercut the whole purpose of giving, which is and always should be to offer help or support unconditionally.

Mastering this kind of giving is a lifelong job. Here's our challenge: At the gym, in the office, at home, and on the freeways, can we start doing things for others as though they had done something for us first? Can we make a habit of acting as though we were the ones repaying the social debt or favor?

When we allow ourselves to keep a "you-owe-me-one" score board, we set expectations that others may or may not know of, or be willing or able to accept. But when we give willingly and openly in as many aspects of our life as we can think of—when we give gifts in a way that sets no expectation for a response— we get something very special in return, something that's beyond economics or etiquette.

Looking for something priceless to give someone? The easiest and best gifts to give are always your own unique gifts of concern, assistance, or reliable moral support. They cost you nothing, you'll never run out of them, and they cannot be bought—only given!

Before you turn the page to Chapter Five, let me ask a few questions. Did you actually complete your goals map? Did you take the time to find the connection between your gifts and your heartfelt intellectual, emotional and financial rewards? Don't cheat yourself from the fulfillment awaiting those who know what gives passion and purpose to their lives. If you've already completed your exercise, I applaud you and your effort. If you haven't, I'll wait right here until you do!

~ Chapter 5 ~

Becoming Unshakably Confident

Confidence is an incredibly important trait, essential, at some level, to success in most aspects of life. In this chapter, you'll learn how to utilize the strongest resource available to maximize your confidence—your own intuition. You'll also learn how to master fear and you'll learn that how you communicate with yourself affects your self-confidence. The chapter concludes with specific confidence-building exercises you can benefit from almost immediately.

Confidence Alert!

- Why don't I just admit it—I don't have the skills. I'll never be able to play in that league.
- Everyone who makes it in this industry has "the right connections"—and I never will.

§ I can't cook. How will I ever make the right impression on Sam's family?

§ That person just hung up on me. I just can't take the rejection part of this job.

§ We'll never be able to find the right home with our limited down payment.

§ I can't go to the dance. I hardly know anyone who will be there.

Warning: a lack of confidence can render your most impressive talents totally ineffective. If your "mental game" is subpar, and if you hear messages that make you feel that it's going to be difficult or impossible to attain key goals, then you're going to have a hard time performing in even a limited capacity.

Fortunately, there is a power that will boost your self-confidence—a power that works while you sleep, guides you when you're lost, and provides confident choices that will lead you to a better and more fulfilling life. This power can give answers to your toughest questions, solutions to pressing problems, and wise and reliable advice when you need it most. This power is your *intuition*—and making the most of it can help you conquer virtually any self-confidence problem. People who use the Power of Will beat the low-confidence trap by developing strong intuitive resources. They know they either already have the right answer to a challenge or that they can find someone who does. In all my years of training, personal success coaching, and public speaking, I've never met anyone who had deep confidence in his or her own intuition and lacked self-confidence.

It's easy to see the reason. A lack of knowledge is the primary ingredient for a lack of self-confidence. We assume we don't know how to respond to a situation, and that we will fail. But our conscious mind is generally only aware of a small fraction of our available knowledge. Some scientists estimate that we typically use less than four percent of what we actually know! People who trust their intuition are able to tap into a larger portion of their "knowledge bank," which includes the subconscious mind, and makes them more confident than the average person.

I firmly believe that by taking full advantage of the sources driving our intuition, we could all have access to a lifetime of knowledge that would help us create unshakable confidence and master virtually any problem.

Just about everyone has evidence of the power of intuition. Haven't you ever had a problem that seemed impossible, but then somehow solved it by "stumbling across" the answer when you weren't really looking for it? Perhaps you were taking a shower, or driving a car, or out running, or simply sitting quietly, thinking about nothing in particular—when all of a sudden, you smiled and realized the impossible problem did have a solution. At that moment, you experienced intuition at work, and you had a fleeting sense of the power of your subconscious mind.

Imagine if you were able to *rely* on that power on a regular basis—if you could tap into this *powerful* resource at *will*!

Well, you can. Lack of confidence is nothing more than an emotional fear that we don't have the experience or skills necessary to resolve a given problem. This may or may not be the case. Our minds are driven by feeling and conjecture more than by hard evidence. Full self-confidence arises with a powerful feeling that we *do* possess the experience and skills necessary, and then use the strength of the subconscious mind to track down the problem-solving answer we need. The idea is to put more than four percent of our minds to work when we face a challenge. This takes practice, but believe me...

~

If I can learn to boost my intuitive powers, anyone can!

~

Your intuition is always at work. It is ever present in your subconscious. Intuitive thoughts occur "without our even trying"—they originate from the subconscious mind. They usually come when least expected, whether we ask for them or not. We all have intuitive power—but we don't always put ourselves into situations where we can benefit from that power.

No Sweat!

Building your intuition powers can be a tricky process at first, because getting your intuition to work wonders should require no *conscious* effort. If you concentrate on the "process" of tapping into your intuition, you actually will hinder your subconscious. It's a passive process. So how *do* you develop this resource? Well, you can do certain things right now to be more receptive to your intuition—actions that will make it easier to listen to what your intuition says.

Bear in mind, as you read what follows, that intuition is a lot like the Chinese bamboo tree. We can plant the seed, and we must care and nurture it for a long time before we can see any obvious signs of physical growth. Then, one day, without warning, it will take off like the space shuttle! There may be a long "incubation" period before your intuition makes its presence known in a more dramatic or predictable way than it already does. Stick with it. Tend the seeds.

Four Things You Can Do to Strengthen Your Connection to Intuition—and Build Confidence

1   *Expose yourself to many facts.* Give your subconscious as many facts and as much information as you can about the challenge you face. The more information you feed your subconscious mind, the more it can help you to move in the desired direction. Let's say I wanted to develop a new educational toy for preschool kids that would make it easy for them to learn different languages. I would give my intuition a boost by reading everything I could about accelerated learning, by taking world language courses, and by surfing the World Wide Web for pages that address this subject. By doing so, I'd increase the likelihood of an intuitive breakthrough.

2   *Learn to focus while in deep thought.* Our minds are naturally restless—but we can learn to focus on questions with clarity and power. Once you can concentrate while

you're thinking deeply about a subject, you'll enter a near-meditative state, sending your subconscious mind the right signals. Please understand that I'm not talking about pushing yourself to memorize or recall material you don't like. The concentration I'm talking about is not anxious, but rather inquisitive on the deepest possible level, and adaptable to any skill level or current state of knowledge. It's the kind of concentration you can use to sneak up on big goals. This type of learning is a little like doing sit-ups. The idea of getting down on the floor and doing 50 sit-ups right now may seem absolutely impossible to you. But if you were to begin with just five right now, and set a goal of adding one more each morning until you reached 50, the goal would be more realistic. Use your deep concentration muscles each and every day, and you'll be an expert in no time!

~

If thinking were a flood light, concentration would be a laser beam.

~

Flex your concentration muscle a little at a time; seed your intuition with information as I mentioned in step one. Then, when you want to bring your information into focus, you can casually call upon the topics or answers you need from your subconscious. Concentrate for five minutes maximum at first, then gradually increase your time to 10 or perhaps even 15 minutes. You might begin by reciting a positive affirmation to yourself: "I am awakening my subconscious to bring me an idea for helping children learn quickly and easily."

Your mind will wander to unrelated thoughts. Expect this, and keep focused. Don't let thoughts distract you. Gently pull your mind back to the task at hand and resume exactly where you left off. Just as sit-ups will eventually have an effect on your tummy muscles, your concentration will begin to effect your mental energy, and you'll soon feel more alert and active as you pursue goals.

3 *Identify your most enjoyable solitary activity.* It doesn't matter if it's surfing, taking a bubble bath, reading by candlelight, or walking through the woods. Find out what gives you inner peace and joy at the same time— then do it on a regular basis!

The search for this activity can be fun. It might take you back to childhood or toward what you've "always wanted to do." However you identify the solitary activity, use it as an intuition "booster."

At the subconscious level where intuitive powers live, your mind is always working. Day or night, while you're awake or sleeping, it's processing information. But it will be more inclined to share results with you when your conscious mind is relatively calm and diverted toward another activity.

Find something you can do on your own, and then keep a pen and paper, a tape recorder, or a piece of drawing paper close at hand. When I decided to write this book, I began to tape-record my speeches. My presentations served as the basis for each chapter. I extended my recordings by carrying a small microcassette recorder on all of my runs. I would describe the vistas as I recorded my inner thoughts. After my runs, I would send the tape to a transcription service. At times, when I retrieved my transcriptions, I would find a note attached: "Thanks for the guided tour! And the insights!"

4 *Think positive thoughts!* Encourage your mind and sub-conscious to focus on positive outcomes. Be supportive and noncritical of your mind's processes. There is nothing more devastating to intuitive powers than to "fire-hose" your own subconscious with negative messages like "This will never work," or "I'm wasting my time."

Eliminate negatives from your mind—and from your life! If that means changing your job, finding new friends, or avoiding contact with certain family members—do it! If you cannot get away from that person or event, then attempt to control, minimize, or influence the negative impact on your outlook and intuition.

Your subconscious mind will "feed back" whatever you feed into it—so be sure you're feeding it the right stuff! Make a conscious choice to include more positive words in your self-talk: "energized" or "excited" rather than "concerned" or "overwhelmed"; "challenged" or "growing" rather than "rejected" or "failing"; "surprised" or "astonished" rather than "puzzled" or "shocked": "I've made the decision to ..." rather than, "I have to..."

You have to make a conscious effort to send positive messages, *because it's so darned easy to send negative ones.* You can still send messages that illustrate negative *consequences,* but be careful not to denigrate yourself or your world in the process. Let me give you an example of what I'm talking about. My dad, who loved me dearly, had a different parenting style than my mom. He'd look out the window and see me playing with friends and say, "What's the matter with you? Are you crazy? Stay out of the street!" The association: "I'm bad! I'm crazy! I don't have enough sense to stay out of the street!" My dad would say (okay, yell) things like that because he was concerned about the danger I was in, and he wanted to make sure the message got across. So, he picked a way of getting my attention that he thought I couldn't ignore.

My mom took a positive approach—and one with a more pronounced long-term effect. To teach me that busses and cars on 14th Street in Hoboken, New Jersey weighed tons, and wouldn't always be able to see a small kid running out to the first base manhole, she took me to the park, sat me down, and said, "Son, you're a smart boy." The association: "My mom knows a smart kid when she sees one!" Then she said, "I want to talk to you about where you boys play your stickball games." She directed my attention to an ant crossing a small patch of asphalt.

She pulled out my dad's 16-pound bowling ball—I'd been wondering why she brought it—and she dropped it on the ant. Dead ant! From that point, my association was "the street is bad," and "ants can't hold up bowling balls."

Guess which message changed the way I played each afternoon? Guess which message left a "picture" in my mind? My mom knew what my dad didn't. That I was a "visual" learner, not an "auditory" one.

Building Trust in Yourself

Don't think of your intuition as something that's either "right" or "wrong"—think of it as a huge library of personal information, experience, and previously unnoticed wisdom you can have at any time. Use this resource to remind yourself of important past experiences, current strategies, and relevant values and beliefs. You'll have a superior confidence-builder you can use at any time.

Sometimes your intuition will point strongly in a particular direction. Sometimes the feeling you get about a certain course of action won't be as strong, and you'll want to validate the strategy by appealing to an outside source, modifying it to fit your objectives more closely, or perhaps even rejecting it. After a while, your intuition will establish a track record. You'll learn when it can be trusted without question—and when the level of certainty is below your need.

Side Benefits

In addition to building up your confidence in yourself, I think you'll find that listening to that "still small voice" will also make you a better, stronger, more intelligent, and happier person.

The courses of action you settle on will, as a rule, lead you to favor situations featuring delayed gratification over short-term, immediate payoff situations. This is good—though it may take time to get used to having "dessert after dinner," rather than the reverse. Be forewarned—in many situations, your instinct will point toward a different mindset than that adopted by our hurry-up, mass-consumption, charge-it, get-the-payoff-now culture. Over time, if you practice listening to your intuitive voice, you'll learn the benefits of thinking in a different way.

Your intuition may tell you things nobody else will. Whatever message your intuition sends, remember one simple fact: Your interpretation of any situation matters. Using the information from your intuition counts the most in the long term. So take action! Once you've identified an area where you haven't been as committed as you should have been, *make it difficult to put off steps that will lead to positive growth in that area.* My favorite strategy here is to "go public" with a goal or plan my intuition has brought to my attention—particularly if it's a goal I should have acted on before. Share your plans—tell your brother-in-law, colleague, the local librarian, or anyone you can think of, that you're going to take a language course to help launch your new educational toy. Don't be afraid to take intermediate steps. Remember, base hits turn into runs, and runs can add up to a winning score.

Another benefit of boosting your intuitive power is opening up your intellectual horizons. You'll be more likely to build productive alliances with other people. This happens because your intuition will sometimes (gasp!) provide more questions than answers. Finding answers to these questions and making decisions can leave you feeling stuck. But this is a good kind of stuck; it's encouraging you to learn and grow and find out more about the situation. The answer here is a time-honored one: assemble a board of advisors—either official or unofficial—to help obtain the advice you need.

Every successful organization has individuals who pool their combined knowledge and assist in the guidance and growth of the organization. These groups have many names, and the individuals who sit on the board offer different backgrounds, levels of experience, and education, but they all have one thing in common...

~

They believe in the cause.

~

Using other people's brains to augment your own improves confidence levels—big time! You may ask yourself: "Why would anyone want to help me make decisions and become a greater success?" Well, you wouldn't want just "anyone" helping you. You must search for individuals who like, trust, and believe in you. Use people you have helped, people you respect and admire, and (perhaps most important of all) people who can help you. If that sounds like a tall order, it is. But your confidence and future is worth it. If you face decisions that require more than one person's store of conscious and unconscious knowledge—and you will—recruit additional members for your board of advisors. Look in all areas of your life: your family, your customers, your place of worship, or your professional network. Tap all possible resources and keep digging until you track down people who have knowledge, commitment to you as a person, and a belief in your cause.

I believe self-confidence arises from self-trust, and that self-trust means trusting yourself above everyone else. It *doesn't* mean that you can't ask for advice or help! Seeking other opinions and assistance, and examining their answers and advice, is evidence of a *high* degree of self-trust.

Don't Expect Perfection

Your intuition has flaws. Remember, it's human! Perfectionism and self-criticism have no place in your emerging relationship with your intuition. Banish them from your mind! Accept wrong moves as learning experiences and move on. There is risk in every new undertaking, new idea, and new relationship. Add the information to your "files" and accept that your "computer" became a little smarter.

⁓

The only mistake you can really make is...
not making any mistakes.

⁓

Very little of what we do is ever evaluated as though it were essential to be absolutely perfect. Yet, many people find it necessary to turn self-criticism into paralysis by demanding that all their final results be perfect. That's an unrealistic standard, and if indulged too much, it will cripple your intuition!

When I was a youngster, my family had an old boat named Dinky; it was my pride and joy. My dad and I worked hour after hour each spring (and most of the year) getting Dinky shipshape. We weren't great ship builders, and we left our fair share of gaps and spaces in the woodwork. Every time we'd notice a gap (and there were quite a few) my dad would say, "Don't worry about it—we'll just put a molding on top of it!" He'd always have a good laugh when he said that, and he'd make me laugh, too. We always moved on to the next woodworking job the boat required and we spent a fair amount of time fitting moldings on top of moldings, covering up imperfections. But it floated!

Is there a time when you have to be passionate about quality? Sure. But you can't be so passionate that nothing ever happens! I've got many fond memories of hot summer days cruising up and down the Hudson River on Dinky. No naval architect in the world could establish a dollar value for the precious memories or the time I spent on Dinky with my father, molding or no molding.

To this day, when something isn't quite right, but it gets done, and progress toward an important goal is not impeded, my family will hear me say, "Don't worry, we'll just put a molding on it." Guess what? Life isn't supposed to be perfect! I believe, when the final speech is given, I will not be judged upon how perfect I was or how many moldings I used, but rather on what I've accomplished and what I've given back during my "tour of duty." As you work to develop a stronger, more effective intuitive sense, be sure to think in a long-term mode, and do not demand perfection from your subconscious each and every time you ask it for help.

Dealing with Fear and Despair

Looking for a great way to undermine your self-confidence? Attend a fear-and-despair seminar.

"Ladies and gentlemen, please take your seats. Our program will begin in five minutes." There was a final flurry of pushing and shoving for seats and elbowroom in the massive auditorium before the crowd began to quiet down. The house lights dimmed, and spotlights brightened the podium. A voice issued from the PA system: "And now, Downer Productions is pleased to present the greatest master of failure, the only person you'll ever meet who can take a winner and show that person how to be an instant loser—Dr. Ima Looser!"

The crowd nearly blew the roof off the place when the good doctor took the stage. People joined arms and chanted the title of the self-destruct guru's two latest books: "GET SCARED! WE'RE ALL DOOMED! GET SCARED! WE'RE ALL DOOMED! GET SCARED! WE'RE ALL DOOMED!" Clearly, these people were motivated. They had paid 68 dollars each for the privilege of learning how to cripple self-confidence and short-circuit their goals. It was evident that they intended to get their money's worth.

Sound a bit far-fetched? Perhaps. But with all of the negativity in the workplace and at home, it surprises me that someone doesn't capture the marketplace and develop a self-help (or should it be self-hamper?) seminar on the subject of building fear, to increase uncertainty and failure. There's obviously a market for this stuff!

How many people do you run into who are paralyzed by fear? I'm talking about the chronic "negaholics" who shy away from every growth experience and build their bad luck from scratch. When there's a setback, they tell their family, "See, I told you I was unlucky! Don't ever ask me to try anything new again!" If something good happens to them, they say "Dumb luck! That will never happen again." These same people have their share of "medical" problems, too. Chronic headaches, lower back pain, knee problems, allergies, and a host of maladies. Like a magnet, they attract bad "happenings" and circumstances.

If your mind is preoccupied with pleasurable, healthy thoughts, then your body will attempt to generate a healthy existence. If your mind is full of negative thoughts and emotions, then health problems are likely in your life. The more intense the negative emotions, the more severe the health consequences could be. Having a negative attitude takes more energy than having a great attitude, and being negative causes stress. Stress puts a serious strain on your heart and other organs.

Maybe reading paragraphs like the one above leaves you feeling skeptical, as though I'm spouting New Age nonsense to sell crystals and turnip extract oil that you can use to examine and polish your aura every night. Actually, scientific studies have validated the idea that your mental state has a profound impact on your physical well-being, and that spending most of your time feeling frightened and in despair is bad for you. A 12-year study found that of 2,328 middle-aged men and women, those who felt endless despair had a heightened mortality rate from heart disease. And for the small percentage who were most severely depressed, the death rate from heart disease was four times greater when compared to the rate for those with no depression!

If a fearful or despairing attitude can have such a strong effect on your body, is it really so much to think it can affect other elements of your life?

I'd Like to Be Confident—But this Situation Scares Me!

Many people at my seminars tell me, "I know I shouldn't be frightened of doing so-and-so... I know the only way I'm going to be able to grow is if I move past this fear... but for some reason, I can't!" I think it would be more accurate for them to say that they've become accustomed to the results of having a certain fear, and they don't really have that big a problem with it. If they were seriously motivated to face the fear, they wouldn't be talking about what they "should" do. They'd say, "I *have to* get over my fear of so-and-so!"

Why do so many individuals let fear and despair guide—or rule—their lives? I don't know the answers, but I know this: Despair is rooted in fear, and you can unlearn virtually any fear that you learn.

Ready for a surprise? There are really only two "built-in" fears. Every child is brought into this world with two and only two natural fears: the fear of loud noises and the fear of falling. That's it. Every other fear has been learned—and is the result of training or conscious choice. Fear does serve a purpose—it helps us avoid situations that our brain decides are dangerous or might lead to danger. But you know what? Sometimes our brain is wrong and we're best served by trying to "reprogram" it to learn a new set of associations for a given situation. Here are 14 great ways to overcome a fear. If you work through all 14 ideas, giving each an honest try, and *still* fear a given situation, then the fear may involve something you should see a therapist about—or it may involve loud noises or the prospect of falling!

When fear is about to paralyze you from doing something you want to do and know you should do—something that's not physically dangerous or hazardous to your health or anyone else's—use the strategies below. The first two ideas, which are good for dealing with specific fears, come from my godfather, Uncle Frankie, one of the guiding lights in my youth. Try them first. They have delivered superior results more or less instantly for me and many people I've worked with over the years.

Confidence Builder #1: Lie

That's right, lie. When you're confronted by a fear you know is irrational and rooted in fantasy, don't fight the fear message. Tell yourself the fear is real—it's formidable—and that you must take action.

It sounds silly, but it works like a charm. Lie to yourself about the origin of this fear. Confirm assumptions you've been asking yourself to make, and then (this is essential) *figure out what you have to do as a result.*

Let's say that I've got to give a presentation to the president of the company and her entire staff. I have a sizable fear that this is a do or die situation. I've never given a top-level presentation before! What if they don't like me? What if they don't connect with my topic? Suddenly, I'm paralyzed. Before I know it, I'm developing 50 "worst-case" scenarios, rather than working on my presentation.

It's time to lie about my fear. Instead of conjuring up these vague fears, one after another, I should take on each one in sequence. I should make each fear real in my mind *before* I start fantasizing about any more.

Fear: "They won't like me!" *Response:* "You're right, they won't like you. Knowing that, ask yourself what you can do to change that situation. Should you understand more about each of the participants before giving the presentation? What kind of personalities do they have? Are they Drivers, Analytic, Expressive, or Amiable? Where did they get their education? What hobbies or activities do they enjoy? What do their spouses or companions do? What has to happen before these people listen to the presentation and say, 'Hey—I like this person?'"

Fear: "They won't connect with my topic." *Response:* You're absolutely right—they won't. Do you want them to connect with your topic? If the answer is yes, then you'd better make sure that you've picked a topic that works for your audience. How do you do that? Test-drive it! Dial into their agenda! Send along a questionnaire, or call ahead and interview key people over the telephone. Get opinions about your topic—and fine-tune it or change it if the feedback confirms that people won't connect."

Confidence Builder #2: Steal

Steal every bit of power and energy from your fear by taking action. It's hard to be scared when you're actually doing something (unless you're jumping into a pit of snakes). Render the fear as useless as a screen door on a submarine! Take control of the situation and channel the energy you're currently spending being afraid into developing a plan that will help you learn more about the situation and change it for the better.

Once you devise a plan to steal power from your fear, you become stronger. You start to see your fear as a tiny obstacle. And all you have to do is plan a step-by-step process to implement over a specific time period. Let me give you an example.

A single mother, Edith, feared that her teenage son, Jason, would get involved with gangs and drugs. Jason's new school had a reputation for a lax attitude toward discipline, and there were many troubled students. Edith had to steal every bit of power from her fear, and she did it with a tactical plan. It was March; she had three months before summer recess. She had to act fast. She set up her plan, made some phone calls, and set aside a time for a Jason to accompany her on a special "field trip."

One rainy Saturday afternoon she took Jason to the premature birth wing of a local hospital. She wanted to show him what cocaine can do to innocent people. They walked through the wards filled with babies born addicted to crack cocaine. The boy never forgot what he saw.

Next, Edith took Jason to the rehab center for patients with spinal cord injuries—most would never walk again. On the way, Edith showed Jason an article reporting that over 70 percent of street violence involved guns, and that of the injuries caused by gunshots, 67 percent were irreversible spinal cord injuries. In the ward, Jason gasped as he saw teenagers who were lucky to be alive and who would probably remain paralyzed, never play basketball at the school gym, and never dance at their high school prom. Edith's last stop was the hospital administration office. Prior to their visit, she had inquired about the possibility of Jason becoming a volunteer at the rehab center during summer vacation. As Jason filled out the application, Edith knew she had stolen every bit of power from her fear—and given it new energy in the form of a plan that resulted in education for Jason and help for people who needed it.

Confidence Builder #3: Change Your Setting

Sometimes a change of scenery will help eliminate negative self-talk and help you tune out negative voices and the fear they produce. If your environment is causing you to build unhealthy fears, do your best to change your surroundings and start from scratch.

Confidence Builder #4: Share What You Know

Take time to help someone overcome one of his or her fears—especially if you can relate to it and help analyze it. Hey, sometimes it really is easier to give advice than to take it, and sometimes you're smarter for having given advice! Often, teaching others helps *us* to learn or reinforce key lessons, and it certainly can boost your confidence level.

Confidence Builder #5: Learn to Give Compliments

Don't just assume that your subordinates, coworkers, and family members know you appreciate them. *Tell* people when they've done a good job. Better yet, call their parents, spouse, or their boss and tell them, too. Suddenly, you'll feel like a superhero—and the person you're praising will feel pretty good, too!

Recently, Mike, our graphic designer, was in the office with his lovely wife. I took the opportunity to tell Mike's wife that I thought he was a genius and that his work was spectacular. He beamed as his wife smiled and said, "I know!"

Confidence Builder #6: Learn to Take Compliments

When someone says, "Great job!" don't reply with, "Oh, it was nothing." Instead say: "Thanks for recognizing it, I did work hard on that project." When a child or someone you care for says, "Thank you," make eye contact! Look at the person and say something like "It's wonderful that you've taken the time to thank me, and it really makes me feel great!" When you accept a compliment sincerely, you also compliment the person giving the compliment! Now, that's a perfect win/win situation!

Confidence Builder #7: Take on the Tough Job

At some point during the next 30 days, tackle one unpleasant task that you've been avoiding. You'll learn how to face tough situations, and you'll learn how to flex the emotional muscles that help you accept change and fight fear.

Confidence Builder #8: Schedule Quiet Time with Yourself

Over the next 30 days, spend at least 30 minutes every other day in silence with yourself. Don't read the newspapers or watch TV; spend quiet time on your own by walking or running or simply sitting quietly someplace. Get in touch with your own innermost thoughts and intuition—figure out what's on your mind!

Confidence Builder #9: Give the Evening News a Rest

For a solid month, skip the evening news. These broadcasts feature too much pain, paranoia, and emotional exploitation! If you want to find out what's happening in the world, read the newspaper.

Confidence Builder #10: Make a "Can Do" / "Can't Do" List

Place all your worries and concerns on this list by category. Any worry you have some kind of control over goes under "can do"; all of your "useless" worries go under the "can't do" column. Be honest! Fears are worries that are left to fester and grow without reason. Resolve to abandon at least one "can't do" worry from your list; shed it from your life and emotions forever.

Confidence Builder #11: Rent a Marx Brothers Movie

Or read a great book of jokes. Or hang out with a friend who makes you laugh. Whatever you do, find reasons to laugh and be happy. It is physically and emotionally more draining to frown than to smile—so give yourself a break!

Confidence Builder #12: Let Go of Something that Has You Steamed

Yeah, I know, it takes practice. Try it, though. If someone cuts you off in traffic, see what happens to you emotionally when you wish that person well, rather than mutter about the person's lineage! Don't point—wave as the other person goes on his or her merry way. New rule: If you hold a grudge, you lose, and the other person wins.

Confidence Builder #13: Pick Up the Tab

Find the most positive, optimistic person you know. Take that person to lunch, or perhaps play a round of golf or handball together. Make every attempt to associate with upbeat people—not deadbeat people.

Confidence Builder #14: Stand Your Ground

Stop being an emotional victim! If someone uses you as a door-mat or as a mental dumping ground more than twice, you're allowing that person to mistreat you! Take this power away from anyone who is abusive to you or the people you love. Draw appropriate limits and enforce them by *not rewarding* abusive behavior: "You know what? We've got to find another way to discuss this, because I don't respond well when you talk to me that way."

Use these ideas to build up your self-confidence. Wipe fear and despair out of your life and the lives of the people you care for. Remind yourself that whenever the opportunity arises, that you were meant enjoy your short ride on Spaceship Earth.

I Don't Like Mushrooms

"I hate and detest mushrooms."

"Oh, go ahead and try one anyway."

"Nope. No, thanks. I'm quite sure about this. I don't like them. I am totally confident that I wouldn't enjoy eating mushrooms, as confident as I've ever been of anything in my life."

"Have you ever tasted one?"

"No."

"Then how do you know you don't like them?"

"My mom used to make me eat them when I was a kid. Hated 'em then, hate 'em now."

"But I thought you said you'd never tasted them?"

"I never have. I'd just stare at them until she took them away. Just the sight of them turns me off."

We're often supremely confident that we "don't like" one thing or another—even when we have little or no experience in the area in question. It starts with foods like mushrooms or spinach. As young adults we may pile other things onto the list.

§   I don't like museums.

- 𝄢 Classical music is a bore.
- 𝄢 There's nothing to do at so-and-so's house.
- 𝄢 I hate the opera.
- 𝄢 I could never be a salesperson (small business owner, scientist, politician, etc.).

Beware of the mushroom effect! This "anti-confidence" sets up patterns of mistrust and negativity, and leaves no room for new experiences to take shape. Our brains get used to saying "No" instead of "Why not?" Before too long, just like a mushroom, you'll feel as though like you're always in the dark.

These days, I' am on a mission to catch myself in the act of being "anti-confident." I have vowed to take a bite, look up the new word, take the ride, cook the recipe, and go on the trip. Instead of saying "Oh, I'll just wait here, you kids go ahead and do it," I've decided that I have to get into the picture—not just take it—when it comes to things I've decided (based on little or no evidence) that I don't like. Why? Because I want to take everything in my life to the next level! That means building confidence that I am capable of doing anything I want to do. And that kind of unshakable confidence starts with an open mind!

Of course, there are still exceptions: places I haven't yet traveled, prejudices against new experiences I haven't yet uprooted. But my list of automatic "No" answers is getting smaller every day.

Here, have a mushroom!

~ Chapter 6 ~

Energy Sources

There are many different kinds of energy: mental, physical, intellectual, spiritual and emotional. In this chapter, you'll learn strategies for increasing each kind of energy—and reap substantial life benefits as a result.

Mental energy is the "hub" of all energies; internal conflict is the greatest source of low mental energy. In the following pages, you'll begin to explore important questions about your own level of mental energy: What internal conflicts are taking place in your mind? What are the main motivators creating these conflicts? What steps can you take to increase your energy level in other areas?

The Power of Will and Mental Energy

People who make the Power of Will a daily reality are like power generators—you can sense the "juice" radiating from them when you shake their hand or hear them speak. Think about when you met the last person who truly inspired you. Didn't you feel great for hours, days, or even weeks afterward? It was like you were hooked up to a million-watt generator for a couple of minutes! These people have abundant positive mental energy.

How do they pull it off? They use their mental attitudes to develop true consistency in their lives and their energy levels rise in many areas! People who talk the talk and walk the walk are superior overall energy sources. They are completely in tune.

As you'll recall from Chapter One, taking full advantage of the Power of Will means you act exactly as you believe. These "power station people" encounter little or no wheel-spinning, internal conflict, or tug-of-war. They waste virtually no mental energy, meaning they usually have ample intellectual, spiritual, emotional, and physical energy. Their systems all work in full synchronization and harmony.

Can you become one of these people? Sure you can. Just learn how to make what already happens sporadically in your life happen regularly.

If you think back, you'll probably realize that you have experienced similar moments of peak energy, times when you felt your entire mind, body and soul work toward a particular goal or desire. The only real difference between you and the "power station person" is that you probably stumbled into this state of balanced, focused energy efficiency, while the person who makes it a way of life knows how to make it work on a regular basis.

Different cultures have different names for this feeling of complete and balanced connection. In Japan, they call it "satori;" in America, I've heard it called being "in the groove" or "in the zone." Whatever you call this integrated, completely focused state of consciousness, it boils down to efficient collaboration between your mind, body, and soul.

When you're "in the zone" (to use what's probably the most familiar American term), you're like a business operating at absolute peak efficiency, with perfect teamwork from all employees and all members of the management team. You're humming.

You're as productive as you can possibly be, as "in tune" as you'd feel on the best day of your life. Everything is clicking!

Stop the WAR!

WAR= Worries, Anxiety, and Regret

These are the three major energy zappers on the mental front. They are so dangerous, so likely to take you "out of the zone," that we should look at each in appropriate detail.

Worries

Are you looking for a great way to exhaust your entire energy system? If you are, just keep worrying about the "stuff" you normally worry about on a daily basis. Worrying makes you tired! If you've ever wondered why you felt exhausted after a difficult day, even without performing strenuous physical activities, the answer is almost certainly that you were worried or stressed out.

Originally, the phrase "to be worried" meant "to be torn apart, as by wild animals." Over time, the metaphoric use of this idea turned into a primary meaning: to be apprehensively concerned about something. If you stop to think about it, you'll realize that the original association is appropriate! When we worry instead of taking action to fix problems... when we make a habit of worrying about the same things on a regular basis... when we worry about things that always or usually turn out for the best... then, we tear ourselves in pieces!

I estimate that 75 percent of the things people I work with worry about simply never happen. If you think that estimate sounds high, feel free to make a list of the last 30 things you worried about, and check the figures yourself. Be sure to include *every* recent worry—even minor ones. If you find that more than seven of the things that concerned you did transpire essentially as you had imagined they would, then please contact me! I could use a good clairvoyant!

It also seems fair to estimate that, of the things we worry about that *do* take place, at least half are situations we can't control. That makes that slice of the "worry pie" 12 and a half percent wide, which leaves only 12 and a half percent of our worries connected to scenarios that actually take place and that we have some control over—and even these are likely to occur in far less terrifying and intimidating ways than we may initially imagine.

Typically, when we worry, we bring our deepest, darkest concerns to the forefront of our minds—which is a bad place to leave them! When we do, we may feel that we are at least "focusing" on a particular problem, but we may be doing more harm than good. As complex and powerful as it is, the human brain cannot concentrate on the opposite of an idea or suggestion. In other words, when you worry about a negative potential outcome, your mind will only see the outcome that you're trying to avoid. (Remember, if your mind can see it, it can do it!)

Thirty-five years ago, my father tried to talk me through the instructions that would help guide our boat Dinky safely into dock. Unfortunately, his instructions only focused on the negative possibilities: "Don't blow it, son... Don't hit the dock... Steady as she goes, now, you're turning too much... Don't get too close to the pilings..." Guess what happened?

You got it. The first piling I hit took out the third porthole on the starboard side. That piling had an exposed spike that gouged about three-quarters of an inch from a five-foot section of mahogany planking. The boat was a mess, and so was I. Although it wasn't one of the most enjoyable experiences I had on a boat with my father, I have to admit that it certainly was among the most memorable.

Not long ago, I found myself in a similar situation—except now, I was doing the coaching: My young friend, Stephanie, was at the wheel. Remembering my experience with my father, I made a conscious effort to help her focus on the positive outcome we both wanted. "Picture the boat safely tied along side the dock," I suggested before we started." You'll want your approach to be slow, with the bow pointed right at the center of the dock. You'll feel a slight nudge as you stop, right in between the two bumpers. Once you feel that, you'll know to put the engine in reverse, and you'll have a perfect landing. I know you can do it."

Do it she did! When she executed this feat of nautical naviga-
tion, Stephanie was enjoying her first boat ride. That's right, she
had never been on a sailboat, much less held the wheel of a 42-foot
sloop. But Stephanie came through fine, and used the energy
she could have spent worrying to deliver a perfect outcome. I
wish I had a camera to take a picture of Stephanie and her proud
parents and grandparents, who happened to be on the boat!

Ditch Your Worries!

Constant worries clutter our minds and serve as a form of "negative
visualization." They have the real potential to make seriously unde-
sirable results become honest to goodness realities.

What can we do to limit our worries? Here are several tools
you can use to separate worries from likely outcomes.

First, take time out to analyze your current situation. Compare
the hard facts to the assumptions of your perceived worry. How
likely is it that what you're concerned about will really take place?
Has anything similar to what you're worried about taken
place before? Have you ever worried about this particular outcome before and found that your concerns were not warranted?
Use words of entitlement, rather than words of worry, to stop
yourself from repeating a particular worry.

Words of Worry	Words of Entitlement
I could have.	I will next time.
I wish...	I will...
I'll try...	I'll do...
This is too hard.	I'll enjoy the challenge.
I'll never be able to...	Let me give it a shot...
I'm too afraid...	I feel excited...
I fear the worst.	Let's see what's in it for me.

Words of Worry	Words of Entitlement
I feel a bit insecure...	I am going to query my emotions...
I am feeling nervous...	I am feeling more animated...
This is terrible.	This is unlike anything I expected.
The thought petrifies me.	I am going to find out more.
I am embarrassed by...	I am more conscious of what's happening.

Evaluate the Worry Against Your Positive Traits

Ask yourself, "Is this worry in conflict with one of my positive traits? If so, which one?"

Let's say that one of your positive traits is creativity, even when you're working under a very tight deadline or under pressure. You worry about a possible negative outcome associated with a proposal you submitted at work. Or, perhaps you're worried about how you're going to host your relatives during the upcoming holiday season: Where will they stay? Soon, you're thinking of terrible things that could happen if your report isn't well received, or all the terrible things your relatives might say about their accommodations. You deplete precious energy you could use to summon creativity—which is exactly what you need to summon!

Your choice to repeat your "mental movie," to replay the worst possible outcome in situations, will impair your ability to take advantage of that positive trait. Your worries will take power away from your creative ability just when you may need that ability.

Once you realize capabilities that have allowed you to overcome similar past problems, you'll find it easier to accept that worrying will sap energy in an area where you already have significant strengths. If you focus on the worry, you let it win!

If you focus on positive traits and how they've served you in the past, you'll be able to summon them when the need arises.

Do a Reality Check!

Evaluate what will happen if the worst happens. Be ruthlessly honest and brutally realistic: What's the most terrible thing that could happen to you if this worry actually became a reality?

To help you quantify any and all possible impacts, ask yourself the following questions:

§ How will this consequence affect my health, finances, emotions, or relationships?

§ If I'm looking at a monetary consequence, can I put a dollar figure on this potential negative outcome? If so, is this amount of money worth spending this much time worrying about?

§ If this worry were to become reality, what steps would I take to recover? How difficult would it be to establish the status quo, or repair the damaged relationship?

Reach a Conclusion

Use common sense in addressing your worries and their implications. Be open to real-world evidence that what you're worried about is unlikely to come to pass, or less significant than you initially feared. (All too often, we tune out any indications that a particular worry is highly unlikely or even ridiculous.) Above all, don't try too hard to stop worrying! Exerting all your energies to forget your worries will leave you feeling tired, and will only strengthen worries you try to eliminate! Use the energy to set up a plan, if that's really what needs to happen next. Then...

Move On

Refocus your thoughts. If necessary, change your physical posture or environment. Go for a walk or run, clean out your sock drawer, or think about something absurd. Force yourself to take some form of physical and mental time out. This is a simple and highly effective technique for dealing with worries. It is a thousand times more constructive than our first instinct—to build up past negative situations in our mind and find as many points of contact between our current challenge and the past problems we've faced. If we ask our minds to reinforce our worries, they will comply!

Let me reinforce a key point because we lose sight of it so frequently. Few, if any, of our worries are as serious or life threatening as we imagine them to be at the time. When we take time to evaluate our situation objectively, we realize the vast majority of outcomes that arise from situations that once worried us were far better than we had anticipated.

Anxiety

What is an anxiety? It's an intensified worry that occurs despite our best efforts to tame it, and causes prolonged fear and unease.

Anxieties are worries that have moved in and set up house in our minds, even after we've served an eviction notice by trying to focus on something else. An anxiety often leaves you feeling slightly (or maybe not so slightly) out of control of your mental processes—an unsettling experience indeed!

Anxieties may make you feel as though you've been possessed by an outside force. Despite your efforts not to waste energy by focusing on possible negative outcomes, your brain seems to have been hijacked. You feel you have no alternative but to follow it toward the "Adrenaline Triangle"!

You don't require clinical help to solve problems with anxiety! Garden variety "surface" anxiety can make it difficult to think rationally, evaluate simple data, speak or write intelligently, and communicate effectively. In some people, anxieties grow into serious psychological disorders.

The suggestions that follow should not be mistaken for clinical advice for deep-rooted problems manifested in the form of chronic anxiety, such as panic attacks, eating disorders, or other serious problems. If you experience an anxiety-related problem that frequently impairs your normal social functioning, regularly robs you of sleep, or leads to deep depression, you should enlist the help of a qualified professional. If the surface anxieties are of the "Here we go again" variety, you may wish to use what follows and see what happens.

When you find yourself spinning your wheels for 10 minutes or longer as a direct result of an expectation about a troubling, pending situation, use questions to give yourself perspective and stop the anxiety.

- What evidence do I currently have that will support the intensity of this anxiety? Is there any at all? (Most anxieties do not have enough evidence to "stand up in court.")

- What, exactly, do I fear? Is it a particular person, place, situation—or do I find new reasons to be fearful or apprehensive as I shift from subject to subject? (The act of recognizing this pattern, in and of itself, may help you to combat the phenomenon of "free-floating" anxiety.)

- What percentage of this anxiety is rooted in actual events? What percentage of this anxiety is connected to imaginary or hypothetical situations? (Come up with hard numbers— your best estimates. This is a particularly important question; be sure you approach it from a totally honest and open mind. Demand that your mind help you identify all aspects of this anxiety that are rooted in suppositions, fantasies, or imaginary scenarios.)

- When does this anxiety present itself most dramatically to me? (The knowledge that you are likely to feel most anxious at certain times of the day can help put things in perspective.)

- What benefits would I enjoy if I could get rid of this anxiety? (Focus on the positive!)

By asking and answering these questions, you can probably lower the intensity of the anxiety you feel. If you can lower the intensity, you can continue the process and eliminate the anxiety. But you must take the initiative and commit yourself to overcoming this obstacle, or you may find it blocking your path for the future.

Regret

Regret can be defined as a feeling of distress for what is past and lost beyond recall. I think of regrets as mistakes we can't do anything about and we can't seem to escape from. What is the best way to deal with energy sapping regrets? Simple:

~

Regrets should be turned into apologies—
and then forgotten!

~

Regrets lead to unhealthy preoccupation with "What might have been" and endless fixation on past circumstances. We each have a choice: We can dedicate our energies to the present and build a future, or we can focus on the past. When we find ourselves "hard-wired" to regret, we have chosen the past and have chosen to waste precious energy.

Instead of channeling your mental "capital" into past circumstances, lost opportunities, battered dreams, egos, or meditations on what could possibly have saved star-crossed relationships, resume control by taking action. Resolve your regret by making an appropriate apology—to another party or perhaps even to yourself—and then move on!

This apology may or may not be a discussion with another person. What's important is that you take action to make the situation feel right in *your* heart. The objective is to free up your energy for other tasks.

You may never be able to reconcile a regret to win the approval of another person affected by something you did (or didn't do). That's okay. You don't *really* want to define yourself through others, anyway. Just make sure the action you take leaves you feeling as though you've responsibly closed the issue. Your apology may be a phone call, a letter, a gift to a charitable organization, or a period of prayer. You are the final judge in dealing with your own past. Once the apology feels right, do it! Then you can...

Take action on something new and exciting! Dump your regret. Forget about the past, and concentrate on using the present to build your future. The past is gone forever. Don't try to win it back.

Don't get me wrong: memories are wonderful, if we use them intelligently. Use your memories consciously, as a tool to further growth. Use them to connect with people you care about. But don't ever let them use you.

~

The fires that can warm you tomorrow cannot be started with ashes from yesterday.

~

Memories are a part of who we were, but not one single memory has the power to make us who we can be. Only you can ensure that memories point you in the right direction and leave you feeling more energized.

Four More Kinds of Energy

I've examined the first category of energy—mental energy—in some detail, because it affects all the other categories in a dramatic and undeniable way. Let's look at four additional kinds of energy, and some strategies you can use to build up "juice" in each one.

Intellectual Energy

You may have heard it said, "knowledge is power." I believe that knowledge is only *potential* power. Knowledge is like a 500-horsepower engine sitting under the hood of a hot rod. Yep, it's powerful, but until you start it up, put the car in gear, and pop the clutch, you'll never know what that power is capable of doing for you.

~

Intellectual energy alone will not create any memorable or measurable results (other than perhaps a high score on an IQ test).

~

To redeem latent intellectual energy, we must use our intellectual energies wisely. Typically, people fall into one of three categories when it comes to harnessing (or failing to harness) their own intellectual energies.

❀ The people I call "first-stringers" want results and take action to get those results. They often take action before all the facts are on the table. They may fall prey to the "Ready! Fire! Aim!" mindset. Usually, these folks trust the guidance and advice of qualified outsiders and see the inherent risk in any decision process as an opportunity to learn and grow.

❀ The next group is what I call "bench sitters" or "fence sitters." Their perpetual attitude is best described as "wait and see." They want all the evaluations in place before they walk (or, in some cases, crawl) into action. They wait to accumulate an overabundance of knowledge before they leap. They're extremely cautious.

❀ Then there are the "Monday morning quarterbacks." If you're looking for "expert commentators," this is the group to canvass. Bobby Kennedy once said that one-fifth of the people in meetings prefer to vote against everything, all the time. I believe he was thinking of this group. Monday morning quarterbacks have an overabundance of knowledge that makes them outspoken when it comes to opinions and critical evaluations. But when it comes to picking up the ball, they don't.

How can you recognize an opportunity to take action—and take full advantage of your intellectual energy? Here are key points I pass along to seminar participants and others who are interested in the full potential of their intellectual energy:

ʂ Remember, our opinions sometimes need to be changed or updated or take a back seat to new ideas and approaches. Don't mistake opinions for hard facts!

⑟ Consider others' experiences and results; keep an open mind when examining and evaluating how they get things accomplished.

⑟ When you disagree, ask yourself, "What can I learn from this person?" Other people have valid viewpoints, too. Make every possible attempt to find out what's driving the person on the other side. Why does this person have this opinion? Maybe he or she knows something you don't!

⑟ Constantly ask yourself, "How can I do it better?" Asking yourself questions helps boost your creative impulses— which is a wonderful fuel source for intellectual energy.

⑟ Keep a vigilant eye out for new innovations. Open yourself up to new ideas by reading a newspaper every day, follow your industry trade magazine, or hit the Internet for new ideas.

Emotional Energy

If you did a balance sheet, and added up all the positive and negative impacts of emotions you felt on a given day, what would the result be? Would you have excess positive emotions like joy, gratitude, excitement, and good humor—or would you be overwhelmed with negative emotions like frustration, rage, self-pity, and impatience? Would your day conclude with an emotional credit or an emotional debit in your account?

To feel emotionally energized, in control, and in balance, my emotional credits—that is, positive emotions—need to outweigh my emotional debits—the negative emotions—by at least two to one! To track these "transactions," I kept a daily journal. For a month, I kept track of the "balance sheet" in my life. I made a careful accounting of the emotional energy I felt each day, gauging each key situation. After one typical day, my journal looked like this:

DAILY JOURNAL: June 23, 1998

POINTS/RATING

Joy	+10	Rage	-10
Gratitude	+7	Self-Pity	-7
Excitement	+5	Impatience	-5
Good Humor	+3	Disappointment	-3

	ACTIVITY	POINTS	
8:00	Quiet time at breakfast, proofread chapter 5	+10	
	Traffic jam costs me 30 min. Delay!		-5
9:00	Got unexpected call from Johnny	+3	
	Car air conditioner on the blink, HOT!		-3
10:00	Had great team meeting with new salesperson	+7	
	Popped button on my sports coat, embarrassed		-5
	Lost monthly parking permit		-3
11:00	We got the Robertson contract!!!!	+10	
12:00	Lunch with new prospect (very interested)	+5	
	Wrong reservation time at restaurant. Poor choice!		-5
1:00	Surprise e-mail for new speaking date	+5	
	Late pay turns into 5K bad debt		-10
2:00	Publisher says edits on chapter 4 looked great	+10	
	Printer missed delivery–no workbooks for gig		-10
3:00	Brian calls with new promoter opportunity	+7	
	Hutton drops ball on buy		-3

DAILY JOURNAL: June 23, 1998

4:00	Audio album gets free ad space on airlines	+10	
5:00	Mechanic calls; car needs new A/C		-7
6:00	Gym is closed due to water pipe break		-3
7:00	Dinner with friends, fish tacos! Great!	+10	
8:00	Jennifer calls; can make it for Saturday	+7	
9:00	Neighbor calls, dog is lost, needs help		-5
10:00	Sit and read novel by candlelight	+10	
DAILY TOTALS		+94	-59

I strongly suggest that you keep your own emotional "balance sheet" on file as an experiment in maximizing emotional energy. Track your emotions for at least seven days, or for a month if you feel inspired. Use the information to answer the following questions.

⑤ What does your emotional "bank account" look like on a day when you feel hopeful, energetic, and optimistic?

⑤ What positive experiences do you need to make that energizing "end-of-day" feeling happen? How many positive experiences do you need to have?

⑤ What was your greatest emotional high during the time period you tracked?

⑤ What steps can you take to ensure that you have more experiences like that one?

⑤ What was your most significant emotional low during the time period you tracked?

⑤ How can you minimize the frequency or impact of experiences like that one?

There is always room for improvement when finding new ways to earn interest on your emotional "deposits." Look at the following list of strategies you can use to build emotional energy by enhancing your positive emotions and eliminating negative ones.

🏵 Be flexible. Remember, your emotional wealth is at stake! Don't blindly follow a particular course of action or stew endlessly about frustration. If you feel angry or likely to indulge some other negative emotion, use your daily journal entries to identify a similar situation where you found a way to react positively. (Note that I said similar— not identical!) If some computer software aggravates you, do research: What kinds of software do you enjoy using? What features would your current application have to incorporate in order to make this computer task a breeze? What other programs are there—and how much work would it take to replace the software with one that you find easy to use? Take action to change the situation— and don't let negative emotions build!

🏵 Take full advantage of "positive reasons." These are reasons to enjoy being alive. Seek smaller pleasures; indulge them as much and as often as possible. If you derive great joy from sitting in your garden on Saturday mornings, (which, by the way, is exactly where I happen to be sitting now!) capture as much of this positive emotion as possible—and then recreate it! Place a scented candle or some potpourri in your office or workspace to remind you of your garden time. Bring cut flowers from your flowerbed; you can give them to a friend at work, or place them in your own workspace. Take a picture of your garden while it's in full bloom, and place it where you can see it at all times.

🏵 Take full advantage of the "positive seasons." Like the seasons of the year, there are seasons of emotion. You can harness these waves for maximum advantage. Studies of athletes and other people who rely on emotional strength indicate that the ability to initiate a "psyched-up" phase—and thereby initiate a flood of positive emotions— is often a key predictor of success.

Positive Seasons on Demand: Five Tips for Bringing about a Positive "Psyched-Up" Emotional State

§ Learn to relax your mind and body together. Yoga is a great, and proven, tool that will help you—and you don't have to be an expert to enjoy almost immediate benefits. Sign up for a class at your local community center.

§ Forget the specific outcome. When it comes to priming the emotional pump, most people find it beneficial *not* to focus on the desired, specific outcome. In many cases, doing so will only increase stress. If your aim is to "prime the emotional pump," recall emotions you associate with the desired outcome. For example, if you want to win a chess game, drum up the emotions of the win—not the process, tactics, or specific moves you'll have to initiate.

§ Defer self-criticism. You're standing at the "free-throw line" of any situation, and the first shot doesn't go in. You may be tempted to analyze what went wrong in your delivery—but save that analysis for later. You've still got to focus on the second shot! Afterward, when you're in the right frame of mind and not "on the spot," let your "critical self" enter the picture.

§ Build a ritual. Different people have different rituals for achieving a positive emotional state. It doesn't matter whether you make a strange face, snap a finger next to your right ear, visualize yourself in a positive emotional state, give someone a high five, or establish a physical routine that's rooted in repetition (like flipping a coin or writing an affirming statement in your journal). What *does* matter is that you use the technique that works to create the emotional season you want.

Managing our emotional energy is incredibly important. When we do so effectively, we often feel we're soaring, even at the end of an active, hectic day. When we mismanage our emotional assets or allow others to take us "out of our game plan,"—we may feel tired when we should feel fully rested, and feel depressed and stressed out even when we've got reason to be joyous and grateful. My experience working with people one-on-one and in seminar settings leads me to believe emotional energy is the easiest kind of energy to control; it can be reversed in a heartbeat—when people make a conscious decision to do so! (Try this exercise yourself right now: Go into a private place, take on a positive posture, and say to yourself, with conviction: "I'm going to feel good, right now, for no particular reason." Repeat this phrase 10 times—and see what happens!)

Spiritual Energy

In an earlier chapter, we chose certain words that described who we were and what we stood for. We also agreed that important parts of any practical sense of spirituality are knowing and being true to ourselves. It follows, then, that when the behaviors, personalities, and traits we show to others are identical to who we are inside, we reinforce spiritual energies.

～

Spiritual energy is being who you say you are and doing what you say you'll do.

～

In my view, there are two essential prerequisites to building and sustaining spiritual energy: honesty and integrity.

Honesty

Honesty is one word we understand intuitively, but may have a hard time defining precisely. If honesty means simply telling "the whole truth and nothing but the truth," then why do we feel so good when we tell a child about Santa Claus or the Tooth Fairy? Why do we feel that we're doing "the right thing" when we compliment a new colleague on something trivial (or nonexistent) in order to help him or her build up self-esteem during the first few days on the job? What should we make of doctors who "mislead" their nervous patients by telling them things like, "You've got a great attitude"? When we make a statement that reflects the world as it should be, does that always translate to a "lie"?

There are more pragmatic instances of "deception." "When she calls, tell Mrs. Buddinsky I'm not in." We all tell "little white lies"—some more innocent than others—as a matter of everyday social functioning. For most of us, the question is not whether we will ever make a statement that is at odds with the world around us, but in what context we'll make those statements.

When does a "white lie" become morally troublesome? Here's the best standard I've been able to create:

~

A white lie becomes a real lie when you need to remember what you've said for future reference, or when you tell another lie to cover up the first one.

~

Habitual liars need to develop excellent memories! In many cases, they do. They start out small, with minor exaggerations that appear to be harmless, and then move on to serious deceptions. They get hooked, and may get so used to lying that they lie when it would be to their advantage to tell the truth. Before they know it, they've forged a huge chain of lies. They may even find themselves living out a life of self-deception—"believing" their own whoppers. ("I didn't realize I was supposed to...")

When we get caught in the lying cycle, we cloud and diminish our spirituality. Fortunately, most of us want to tell the truth, and are incapable of making lies a lifestyle choice. If you know and care for someone who can't seem to tell the truth—even if it's in his or her best interest—I encourage you to help that person find professional help. In addition, the following guidelines may be helpful to you.

If You Suspect You May Be Supervising a Chronic Liar

1 Put as many procedures in place as you can to measure this person's output or production on a daily basis. Maintain accurate records of any interactions when you suspect this person may be dishonest.

2 Provide closer than normal supervision.

3 Assign a mentor if you can.

4 Reassign the person immediately if he or she supervises others. (When placed in positions of authority, chronic liars can destroy departments so fast it will make your head spin!)

5 Make sure any and all personnel reviews are delivered in writing and signed by the parties involved.

6 If you have hard evidence of continued deception, theft, or demoralizing behavior, you have a choice: fire the person (check with your legal department first) or make professional help and counseling a mandatory precondition of continued employment.

If You Report to Someone Who You Suspect Is a Chronic Liar

1 Distance yourself from the person as much as possible, and keep appropriate records to document your own honesty.

2 If you love the company, try to get a transfer to another department.

3 If a transfer is impossible, consider updating your resume and finding a different employer.

If You Are Related to Someone You Suspect to Be a Chronic Liar

1 Remember, younger and more impressionable members of the family are likely to mimic the person's values and behavior.

2 Privately confront the person when you discover a lie. Make it clear that you do not regard this behavior as tolerable or acceptable.

3 Do not act as an enabler by making excuses for this person to others.

4 Show how lying or engaging in deceitful behavior is undermining the entire family unit.

5 To the degree that you can, make it clear that each instance of lying or deceitful behavior will have specific consequences.

When we're honest, we don't have to keep track of different stories! All we have to remember is what actually happened. By making honesty a part of our daily life, and encouraging others to do so, we avoid having to defend someone else's web of lies. When we put spiritual energy to work silently and effectively, we deepen the sense of certainty and authenticity that is at the heart of the Power of Will.

Integrity

Integrity is something we earn. Once earned, integrity is easy to maintain and becomes a source of spiritual strength and energy over time. Integrity is rooted in a spiritual understanding of one's personal commitment: when we make a promise to ourselves, or give our word to someone else, we put our integrity on the line.

～

*Having integrity means doing what you can, when you
said you could do it.*

～

The key word is CAN. A simple acronym for that word that will
help you understand how to use your spiritual energy wisely over
time—and strengthen your integrity.

CAN= Capability, Availability and Nix!

Let's look at each in turn.

Capability

People jeopardize integrity by failing to ask themselves a key
question before making a commitment. They should ask, "Can I
do this?"

When you make a promise or conclusive statement about
your intentions, you must confirm that you have the capability
to perform in that area. Say your best friend is ready to move
into a new house. The closing costs have almost wiped out his
family's cash reserves, so they're going to rent a moving truck
and move themselves. They ask for your help. Without thinking,
you immediately agree to help. A week or so goes by, and your
friend calls you remind you of the "moving party" that weekend, and talks about a big oak table that's going to need plenty
of muscle to budge. Suddenly, you realize you shouldn't have
made the commitment in the first place! You have a bad back,
and your doctor wouldn't allow you to lift heavy furniture. (Neither would you, for that matter.) If you had thought about your
physical condition the first time around, you could have explained
to your friend without residual hard feelings. As it stands, you
must now try to back out gracefully from your commitment—
and your friend must scramble to find help on short notice. Your
integrity just took a hit.

Before you make a promise to someone—or to yourself—ask yourself the following questions:

- § Have I ever done what I am promising to do?
- § Have I ever done something similar to this before?
- § Can I imagine myself doing this?
- § If I find it difficult to imagine myself doing this, what would it take me to do this?

If your answers to these questions lead you to believe that you lack the capability to perform the task, you should avoid making a commitment.

Availability

Once you've determined that you have the capability, you'll need to confirm that you are available to do the job. We're not just talking about your social calendar. Are you mentally, emotionally, morally, and physically available for this task?

Consider the following scenario. Your sister-in-law is in a jam. She needs a place to stay for a few weeks while she gets her life in order. She's got baggage—and not just the kind that takes up room in your garage or spare bedroom. She's got an eating disorder, and she's currently undergoing extensive treatment with a physician and a therapist. Should you let her stay? Well, whether you should or not, you do. After all, you tell yourself, this is your spouse's sister. You can't deny her this chance for a fresh start. And yet, as the date approaches, you have serious concerns. You're not sure whether you can handle the responsibility of supporting a person with a complex problem. So you renege. No family member would have faulted you if you'd denied the request initially, but now you've made a bad situation worse by adding unnecessary stress on your sister-in-law—at a time when she doesn't need it. Again, your integrity takes a hit.

The easiest way to check your mental, emotional, moral, and physical availability to do something is to ask yourself the following questions:

§ What will happen if I don't make myself available? (What will happen right now? What will happen shortly before I keep the commitment? What will happen shortly after I keep the commitment?)

§ What are the long-term requirements of this commitment?

§ What are the short-term requirements of this commitment?

§ By making this commitment, will I be making a commitment involving someone or something else later on?

"Nix!"

Sometimes, it's best to cut your losses, maintain your integrity, and simply decline an opportunity or commitment. If you want to keep integrity intact, use this simple, popular slogan to maintain your ability to follow through on commitments:

⁓

Just say no.

⁓

It's no fun to issue a flat, unconditional denial. However, you can use the word "no" to give your message an entirely different meaning. Let me give you some examples. Suppose you were to tell that friend who wants your help with the move something like this:

"Jack, I would love to pitch in and help you with the furniture you need moved, but I can't. I've got a bad back, and I don't think my doctor would be happy with me if I lifted bookcases or tables. I'll be delighted to line your kitchen shelves with contact paper, watch the baby, take care of getting everyone lunch, vacuum the carpets, or do anything else to help out. What do you say?"

And once you've discussed your concerns with your spouse, you might say something like this to the family member who's going through a difficult period in her life:

"Rebecca, I understand that your need is a serious one, and I want to be able to help you land in the right place. But right now, I think we'd all be worse off if you stayed here, because there just isn't going to be the kind of physical and emotional support you need in your life. Let's face it: I'm out on the road all day, and Connie works lots of hours at the post office. We just won't be here that much. But here's what I want to do: I want to sit down and call every person in the family you would feel comfortable staying with, and I want to try to arrange a place for you to stay. What do you say—can you help me put a list together?"

Learning to say "no" in a way that leaves the relationship open for future connection is an art. It takes practice. Once you master it, though, you'll be able maintain integrity—and stay true to your spiritual values by helping people find help where they're more likely to get it. You'll certainly be doing them a favor by being honest about what you can and can't deliver!

Physical Well-Being and Energy

Whether we know it or not, and whether we like it or not, today's high-stress lifestyles eat away at physical energy and health. There is a direct correlation: the greater the stress, the lower our level of physical energy. But when we learn to manage stress effectively, our physical energy and overall health are enhanced.

While sources of stress may be different—news of a disaster, concern over the well being of a loved one who was in an accident, or being hit by a baseball through your living room window—the body's response to stress is usually the same: a chain reaction of protective processes energizing more than 1,400 reactions within the body. This frequently occurs whether or not there is direct evidence for physical harm. Very often, your body reacts as though attacked.

The chemical reactions your brain triggers produce physical changes everywhere in your body. The changes may take the form of increased heart rate, quick intake (and subsequent holding) of the breath, inability to move, sweating, fatigue, muscle tension, and clenched teeth—to name but a few. Stress has a definite physical component. The questions is, how can we manage stress in such a way that our own physical energy is developed to its fullest potential?

Here are a few ideas that can help you get the most from your body's energy. When stress builds, take action while using at least one, and preferably all, of the following tools. However, if evidence of stress overwhelms, and physical tension persists, see a doctor or other professional.

🏵 Stop obsessing and stop striving for perfection. Yes, brain surgeons, air traffic controllers and those in similar positions must commit themselves to a zero material-defect mentality. But they also need to learn when to take a break from the job! An unrelenting quest for perfection in all aspects of your life will shrivel your soul, pickle your brain, and permanently clench most muscles. Demanding 100 percent perfection at all times is a real waste of time, because perfection is virtually impossible. Regardless of your job type, and the life you lead, simply do your best, learn from your setbacks, and move to the next challenge. Don't allow perfection to keep you from experiencing pleasure or from trying new things. You say your form isn't perfect? Who cares! Get out there and run laps anyway. You say your kick needs more power? Who cares! Spend half an hour swimming—it's good for you.

🏵 Take time for joyous personal activities. Don't just say you're going to. Schedule appropriate activities on your calendar. Do what *you* enjoy; don't feel you always need to share these activities with someone. Don't wait until you're companion is available or interested in exactly what you like to do. Find something to do on your own... and make sure you really love it.

🏵 Do the following relaxation exercise. It's a great stress control tool, and it's fun! Sit down in a comfortable armchair. Soften your facial muscles. (The degree of tension you feel in your face affects the tension of your entire body; relax your face and you'll relax your body.) Slacken your jaw. Place your tongue at the bottom of your mouth.

Let your eyes close very softly. Relax your forehead. Let your head rest gently on your hands. Breathe quietly; count your breaths for five minutes or so.

❀ Use positive self-talk. I've made this point before, and I want to make it again because it's so important in reducing stress. We really are a product of everything we put in our minds. By changing your vocabulary, you'll change the messages your brain sends to the body and begin to reduce the number of times per day that your body receives those nine-alarm "Emergency!" messages from headquarters. Learn to use the following positive self-talk phrases:

From	**To**
I am anxious...	Something good is about to happen.
I am depressed...	Let me look for a brighter side.
I dread this...	I feel a bit challenged
I hate...	I would like to...
I am lost without...	I am going to seek a new...

Building Greater Physical Energy and Endurance

Physical exercise produces endorphins, enzymes, and other chemicals that make you feel alive, alert, and awake. When these chemicals are hurtling through your bloodstream, you become more productive, are better coordinated physically, make fewer mental mistakes, and enjoy increased levels of concentration.

The bottom line: Regular exercise makes people feel better about themselves. (It also has a way of turning them into better employees, which is why so many top firms provide recreation areas and on-site exercise facilities.) All the same, no one can *make* you take advantage of any exercise program. Either you're committed to it—or you aren't. It's always going to be you who decides to participate.

Here are some easy steps to help boost physical energy and keep you physically fit.

❀ Make—and keep—an appointment to get a full physical checkup. Ask your doctor what kind of exercise program makes sense for you. Odds are that he or she will suggest a regimen that includes both aerobic workouts, such as sustained walking, running, biking, and swimming, and anaerobic workouts that require short bursts of power, such as weight lifting. After you've discussed your exercise program with your doctor, I strongly suggest that you invest in a heart rate monitor. They're small, inexpensive, and (best of all) fun to use. Ask your doctor what your ideal heart rate should be when you are exercising.

❀ Choose exercise activities that you truly enjoy. For my part, I hate the gym. I love to run. Now, running is an aerobic exercise. I know I need some anaerobic exercise, too. So while I am out running, I carry some small weights and use them to exercise my arms and shoulders. There's an added bonus: the weights make great weapons if some pit bull decides to take up pursuit!

❀ Don't try it alone. Join a club or find an exercise partner. It's much harder to quit when someone you know is watching!

❀ Don't try to do too much, too early. Start slow and build tolerance levels. Don't try to become an Olympian overnight. You will become frustrated, exhaust your muscles, and raise aspirin company stock!

❀ Schedule your exercise periods. Make workouts a part of your weekly routine. Don't skip any sessions! Keep the routine up until it becomes a habit. When a habit is practiced enough, it becomes a skill. When a skill is used enough, you reach a point of mastery. The longer we have a habit, either good or bad, the harder we find it to break! Take the initiative and build the exercise habit. Make exercise a part of your life until it becomes a mastered skill. Once you reach that point, you will feel more alive, and have a great deal more energy, too!

Stop Trying!

"Trying" is just an excuse.

People who haven't developed any effective strategies for attaining a key goal always talk about how hard they're trying. They're trying to loose weight, trying to stop smoking, trying to find the right job, trying to hook up with the right life companion, trying to save money, trying to help the family, trying to visit the folks more often...

Don't you get tired of hearing the word trying? I certainly do! It takes us off the hook. It gives us an excuse for not hitting the mark! It's an all-purpose escape hatch, one that's used all too often. Let's make ourselves a promise, this very minute, to stop uttering the "T" word. Either we're committed to finding a way to *do* something—or we aren't!

Implement this rule for a whole day. I think you'll find that your life will be filled with lots of fresh starts, lots of energy, and lots of purpose. If we'd only tried to get out of bed this morning, we'd still be there!

～ Chapter 7 ～

Self-Esteem

Self-esteem has everything to do with our self-image and nothing to do with the way others view us. In this chapter, you will learn effective techniques for enhancing your own sense of self-esteem—by focusing on the unique assets you offer to yourself and others.

Tiffany's Story

Tiffany is proud of her grades and her ability in school. She is a straight-A student who is well-liked by students and teachers. (In fact, she's class president.) Basically, Tiffany is a bright, well-adjusted kid with a strong sense of who she is and where she's going in life. Discipline problems? None to speak of... until recently, that is.

Yesterday, Tiffany's best friend Sharon broke up with her boyfriend unexpectedly, and then asked Tiffany to skip classes one morning so that she could tell her everything. Reluctantly, Tiffany agreed. She was promptly "busted" by the teacher for cutting class. Tiffany's decision to cut class led to a three-day suspension. Today, the principal forced her to step down from her post as class president. Last but not least, when Tiffany's parents got wind of her decision to cut class, they took away her telephone privileges for four weeks! Tiffany thought to herself, "What kind of world am I living in now?"

Good question! What Tiffany thinks about herself and her responses to situations she now faces will determine the kind of "world" she makes for herself—both in the short and long term. We'll be returning to Tiffany's story later in this chapter. For right now, remember that the sudden change in her surroundings doesn't have the final say on the way Tiffany looks at herself. The *choices* she makes about those surroundings determine her ongoing level of self-esteem.

The Four Pillars of Self-Esteem

The verb "esteem" means "to consider or place value or honor upon, or to regard with reverence." Self-esteem, then, is simply the value we put on ourselves. It has nothing to do with what anyone else thinks or says. The opinions of others may be worth considering if the topic is reputation, or positive word of mouth, or anyone else's response to what you say. But when it comes to the "yardstick" by which you establish an identity for yourself (a very important process!), only your opinion matters. A healthy sense of self (not to be confused with egomania) is essential to tapping into the Power of Will.

Four pillars support our sense of self-esteem—positive or otherwise:

- ♫ Characteristics
- ♫ Expectations
- ♫ Attitude
- ♫ Evidence

Whether we realize it at the time or not, each of life's challenges can add strength to one or more of the self-esteem pillars. Look at each one in detail now.

The First Pillar: Characteristics

Among the strongest factors supporting self-esteem is an inventory of your emotional and physical characteristics. You will get a sense of what's in this inventory by digging deep in your heart and asking yourself questions like: "What do I offer that is special and unique?"

The answer must describe your unique emotional and intellectual characteristics. These characteristics should include your:

- Core Values
- Constructive Beliefs
- Positive Qualities
- Positive Traits
- Opinions
- Convictions
- Personality Style
- Intuition
- _____
- _____
- _____
- _____

By the way, those lines are not typographical errors. I've left you some extra room to add your own important categories for additional characteristics.

Remember, in defining your characteristics, ask questions that yield positive, life-affirming, constructive characteristics. You should ask yourself, "What makes me special?" not "Why won't so and so return my phone calls or go out on a date with me?" Your brain will research any and all questions you put before it! So if you put it to work searching for an answer to a presupposition that is not conducive to your growth and happiness, you'll get lots of answers that drill you into the ground. Instead of building a pillar to support positive self-esteem, you'll weaken or knock down the existing supports!

Now, then. Perhaps you compromise an existing positive characteristic, one that has served you well and is part of your deep personal makeup. If you do, then you automatically devalue yourself. Often, this happens when we attempt to seek the approval of someone whose opinion matters to us, but who really doesn't have our best interests at heart—or perhaps does have our best interests at heart, but can't quite show us in the right way. To win this person over, we cut corners. As easy as it is to fall into this trap, we alone are responsible for compromising our core characteristics. And no one is responsible for reinforcing them except us!

What are the healthy emotional and intellectual characteristics we should support for higher and healthier self-esteem? I believe that they are traits such as curiosity, open-mindedness, and generosity—and such characteristics are rooted in positive underlying values. If you're looking for somewhere to start, start with your values. It is never too late to learn new, constructive values! Here are some strategies to build healthy, more meaningful values that will lead to the development of constructive emotional and intellectual characteristics.

✻ *Find a mentor.* This should be someone you admire who has values you feel are important. What can you do to become more like that person? What steps does he or she feel you should take to improve yourself in a specific area?

❀ *Become an avid reader.* Fiction is fine, but you can turn the great men and women of history into mentors by tracking down their biographies in areas of science, politics, and (if you choose) religion.

❀ *Explore your own spirituality.* Reread Chapter Two of this book. Consider worshipping on a more regular basis; try to build up a friendship with a clergy member. Encourage this relationship as a challenge to improve yourself, while growing closer to the Higher Power in your life.

❀ *Take part in an appropriate evening or weekend seminar.* Identify the value you feel is missing, and commit to the goal of attending a workshop or seminar focused specifically on helping you attain that value. For example, if you hope to improve your ability to act with generosity and respect toward less fortunate people, sign up for a weekend seminar that will train you, in a hands-on way, to serve disadvantaged groups in your area.

A Word about Physical Characteristics

In developing this list of characteristics of high self-esteem, people sometimes get hung up on their physical appearance. They tell themselves that they are too fat, thin, tall, or short—the list is endless. Two pieces of advice can help here.

First, don't list physical characteristics that you do (or don't) like about yourself. Physical attributes are not much help in establishing long-term patterns of positive self-esteem. Second, remember that being attractive to others, which is something many people associate with physical beauty, has a great deal to do—perhaps everything to do—with the amount of self-confidence you project.

I'm sure you can think of some movie star or other person you find remarkably appealing—even though that person is not quite what a Hollywood agent might call "textbook" beautiful. Think of the millions of people who have gone gaga over Barbara Streisand or Humphrey Bogart, and you'll see what I mean.

Unshakable internal confidence in yourself and your mission on earth is the most important component of any physical make-over. If you project a strong sense of truly liking yourself, then your efforts to add some sizzle and flash to the most obvious part of your "package" will probably succeed. But if you constantly look for reasons to be swallowed up by the nearest earthquake fault, then no fashion sense, plastic surgery, or flattering lighting will conceal that internal vacuum for long.

It's probably easier to doubt your physical appeal while interacting with other people (or the mirror on the wall). The following tips will make you feel (and look) great in public. They will help you project confidence, vigor, and vitality no matter what your age or physical attributes. And they're a heck of a lot cheaper than plastic surgery, too!

§ *Walk with a purpose.* Lift your feet, hold your head high and straight.

§ *Keep your spine straight at all times.* When standing, do not lean on or against anything. When you sit, put your butt as far back in the seat as possible. This prevents slouching, radiates positive energy, and reduces possible lower back pain.

§ *Make your handshake fit the situation.* Be attentive to the other person's style and situation. Match your partner's approach: gentle and compassionate, or deliberate and assertive. Don't hold anyone's hand for too long; one to two seconds is appropriate. Make sure your eye contact matches your handshake.

§ *Key in to other people.* Coy glances or insincere compliments—who needs them? Paying complete attention to someone else is the most flattering thing you can do. (The better you feel about yourself, the more likely you are to take an interest in others.) Establish comfortable eye contact, take in everything, and make barrier-breaking statements like, "It's an honor to meet you." If you're talking to someone while sitting down, lean slightly forward—but don't forget, spine straight!

§ *Choose the postures you adopt.* Avoid the "white knuckle" flight posture when sitting. Do something different with your hands and arms. Maybe place one arm on your forearm or rest one hand across your lap.

§ *Focus your energy.* If you aren't consciously choosing to make your hands do something, keep them by your side, in your lap, or in a neutral position. Don't play with imaginary coins in your pocket, click your pen, adjust your clothing, or do anything in the "automatic pilot" category. (Also see the advice on gestures.)

§ *Use positive gestures.* Positive gestures are intentional movements to complement your words and feelings. People with high self-esteem are animated; they use appropriate hand, arm, and facial gestures. The next time you are in a large social group, take a good look at the people. I'll bet that you'll spot individuals with the highest self-esteem using gestures to project themselves and their ideas.

§ *Wherever you are, act like you belong there.* Smile and pretend that you own the place. Survey it as your domain. Yes, you must use common sense with this one, because there are exceptions to this rule: waiting to cross the street while standing in the gutter, say, or attending a wake.

§ *When all else fails, try faking confidence for a couple of minutes.* How would a confident person move from one spot to another? If you look comfortable, you'll start to feel more comfortable. Remember, messages are constantly sent from mind to our body, and from body to our mind, without knowing it. If you make an effort to look the part of a person with high self-esteem, your body will eventually send messages to your mind that will help you act the part.

In addition, you'll want to be sure that your grooming is immaculate, that your personal hygiene is conscientious, and that your choice of attire fits the situation.

The Second Pillar: Expectations

The second pillar of self-esteem has to do with how well we feel we live up to our potential. What do we expect of ourselves? When do we feel we've let ourselves (or others) down?

I think the quickest way to lower self-esteem is by setting unrealistic expectations, falling short, and then taking blame for the outcome.

～

We become what we do repeatedly. If we find ways to win consistently, we become consistent winners.

～

The aim is always to raise enthusiasm so that it is always higher than expectations. It's great to get where you want to go, as long as you have enough energy left to enjoy it. And it's great to set high goals, as long as you realize that meeting your goals should always be an energizing, and not an energy depleting, experience.

Remember, if your goal isn't exciting you, it's not doing the job! Use goals to turn up the volume of your positive thoughts—and turn down the volume of any negative voices playing in your head. Never feel sorry for yourself. When things get tough, remember—someone out there would change places with you in a heartbeat! If you doubt this, take a short detour on your way home tonight and walk the halls of a local hospital, homeless shelter, or clinic. As you leave, you may want to kiss the pavement.

When your enthusiasm is at the highest possible level, you're ready to establish (or reestablish) expectations for yourself. These should be challenging but realistic! Examine the following question:

What do I expect from myself over the next 12 months in the following areas?

§ Recreational

§ Professional

❀ Financial

❀ Personal

Now, before you evaluate any of those expectations in depth, look back. Recall the expectations you had over a similar past period. Which expectations did you meet, exceed, or fall short of? Do you see a pattern? Are you consistently meeting or exceeding expectations in your professional life—but not doing as well in your personal life? Where do you need to change your expectations, enthusiasm, and approach?

Here are some ideas you can use to set reasonable expectations in key areas.

Think of one existing pattern you would change in an area where it has been hard for you to grow. (You might choose to find a way to keep a better eye on your finances.) Focus on ways you could make a modest change that would result in a joyous outcome in this area. Write a list of 10 such steps on a separate sheet of paper. To spur your enthusiasm, link each with a positive, joyous outcome.

❁ From your initial list, identify a step you can take in which you feel you can realistically change for the better within 30 days. This might be as simple as getting a better handle on your finances. You might start by balancing your checkbook to within 50 cents. (Personally, I'd settle for 50 bucks.)

❁ From your initial list, identify a step you can take in which you feel you can realistically change for the better within 10 days. This might be monitoring every expense during that period, and by keeping track of all cash, check, and credit card purchases in a small notebook.

❁ From your initial list, identify a step you can take in which you feel you can realistically change for the better right now. This might be an appointment to meet a Certified Financial Planner at the end of the month to discuss setting up your retirement plan.

Once you've identified three realistic, growth-focused expectations in a given area—use this process to turn them into realities!

Make no mistake: What we expect from ourselves does in fact help establish our sense of self-esteem. If we expect the best, commit ourselves to realistic steps along the way, and make sure that our expectations are driven by enthusiasm, we'll achieve more and grow over time.

Every time your enthusiasm helps you to reach an expectation, you will find more enthusiasm. That enthusiasm will drive your expectations once again. Before you know it, you will have started a chain reaction with the exponential power necessary to transform your self-image and your life—the personal equivalent of harnessing the power of the atom!

The Third Pillar: Attitude

Have you seen the popular line of posters, T-shirts, coffee mugs, and rocks that all bear the following legend in big red letters:

～

Attitude determines altitude!

～

Most people have been taught that it is better to have a "good" attitude than a "bad" attitude. That principle is fine, but it gives scarce meaningful information. I think it encourages too many people to tear themselves down for failing to maintain a "good attitude" when an "alert" or "attentive" attitude would actually be more appropriate.

It's more important—and realistic—to assume the objective of having the best *possible* attitude. This strategy can "upgrade" your own mental outlook, which is the third essential to promoting constructive self-esteem. If someone wielding a snub-nosed .45 handgun robs you, no one will blame you if you try to remain calm, attentive, and careful—rather than establishing yourself as a beacon of mindless good cheer in a dangerous situation. It is not in anyone's best interest to identify positive self-esteem with a commitment to grinning, whether you feel like it or not, and whether it makes sense or not.

You've probably heard many times that "It's not what happens that's important, but how you react to what happens that counts." That's true enough—but how, exactly, are you supposed to take control of your attitude in any given situation? There is a three-step plan to keep your outlook in the "best possible" category. By following the outlined steps, you can point your attitude in the right direction—and keep self-esteem high—in most situations.

Step One: When faced with a formidable obstacle, *carefully observe* your surroundings. This is what we might call a "confirmation" step. We need to look into our surroundings and listen carefully, watch carefully, and perceive carefully. If we don't, we risk feeding our mental computers inaccurate information about the situation. If we are going to react to what happens in the most positive and effective way, and with the best attitude, we should listen intensely, with all of our senses and antennae extended high.

Make the challenge you face the absolute top priority. Have you ever experienced being waited on by a "customer service" person who was talking on the telephone, or engaged in some other way, while ostensibly trying to take care of your needs? The person behind the counter thought it was enough to pay attention to you with half (or less) of his or her available attention. When this person attempted to solve your problem, didn't you usually find that he or she had skipped a step? Well, when we try to respond to two different situations at once, or apply "solutions" before we've had the chance to determine what's really happening, what we're doing is adopting a short-term coping strategy.

Do your best to eliminate all distractions. Give the challenge that you now face your undivided intellectual and emotional attention.

Look and listen for the deepest elements of the incoming message. Ask yourself about the content of this message. What am I supposed to be getting from this? (Take in all the facts!) What emotions are contained in this message? (Be sure you don't omit the emotional content; be sure, too, that you don't allow it to overwhelm you into acting before you should.) Then, ask yourself if any part of this message is misleading, deceptive, or inaccurate. (Identify any possible "information gaps" that have arisen in similar past situations.)

Step Two: Apply your ability to understand this situation. Your first objective is determining what possible impact this situation has, or will have, on your reality. Important: the underlying rule for this step is not to agree or disagree with anything. Don't put up a fight! Just seek to understand. Here are some quick steps to help understand exactly what's going on—without committing yourself to a rush judgment.

Ask yourself why this is taking place. Why is this happening? If the answer points toward something you did (or didn't) do, give that fact appropriate weight before you act.

Ask yourself about the logic and emotions involved. What assumptions, if any, are guiding the other side? How much of a role is another person's emotional reaction playing in this situation? How much of a role are your emotional reactions playing in this situation? This brings us to **Step Three**: Plan your reaction. This is where the rubber meets the road. Select a reaction; never allow it to select you. Your response to this situation is the embodiment of your attitude; your attitude will determine whether you emerge as a "Winner" or "Loser" (self-defined!) in this situation. Ask yourself these questions—first about yourself and then from the point of view of any other people involved in this situation.

- ♪ What impact does this situation have on my immediate future?
- ♪ What personal, professional, or financial consequence will I experience as a result?
- ♪ What results or impact will this situation have on my current expectations?

Based on the answers, try to chart an action course that will positively affect both you and the other person. It's quite possible that you may not be able to meet this objective, but it's certainly worth a try. You'll never be able to control what other people choose to do or not to do—but you, and only you, do have the final say about how you will respond to the situations. Taking into account all that you have determined about the challenge, settle on a single "best" course of action—one that does not needlessly polarize or inflame the situation.

The three-step system we've just examined is simple, painless, and effective. It will help you retain control of your attitude. Practice until it becomes second nature!

Attitude Enhancers

Here are some more quick and easy ways to bolster your attitude— and hold a "best possible" outlook in virtually any situational "weather" life sends your way.

❀ *Help someone you don't know.* Hold a door open, volunteer to carry groceries to someone's car, or (gasp!) let another driver have the right of way. You'll instantly feel better about yourself.

❀ *Schedule personal time on your calendar.* Then use it as scheduled to do something nice for yourself, something that brings you great joy. Believe it or not, spending time being glad you're alive is a great way to keep your attitude pointed in the right direction.

❀ *Make a vow not get overheated about at least 10 "small stuff" problems over the next three days.* Missed your turnoff? No problem—that gives you more time to listen to that inspirational tape you just bought. The law of averages dictates that some of the time we'll screw up; some of our choices won't pan out; some of our instincts will be off; some of our goals won't be fulfilled. Ask yourself what you could have done to make a better decision. (Eight times out of ten, you'll find that you should have gotten better information—for example, a better map.) Make an effort to learn something, anything, from the experience—and then move on!

The Fourth Pillar: Evidence

Evidence is defined as "an action or statement that proves or establishes a strong probability that something has happened." As in a court of law, evidence can be manipulated or presented in many ways.

We constantly gather evidence to support or undermine key assumptions about ourselves. When a strong thought or emotion surfaces, it effects the way you value yourself. When you act on that thought or emotion, you stand a good chance of reinforcing it, which can be either good or bad.

Are we making an effort to focus on the evidence in our lives that supports our best and highest selves? For most of us, there are times when we're tempted to develop evidence that confirms the worst about ourselves ("I missed the FedEx drop-off—I'm always late, what a dummy I am!" "I can't get my hair to look the way I want it to and this outfit is not my color. I'll never be able to make a good impression on Charles.") The challenge is to survey the evidence, make intelligent choices about the messages we send about ourselves, and make the best positive case, without engaging in self-delusion.

We need to make a habit of arguing in favor of our potential to be the person we hope to become. ("I missed the FedEx drop-off—but at least I got the project right. I care so much about the details that I'm willing to drive the package to the airport, rather than send something off without double-checking my facts." "Charles is my kind of guy—he'll appreciate me for how I act, not how I look.")

The aim should be to rethink our "truths" and reapply our best core values and beliefs—so we can restate our evidence before we allow instinctive reactions to new situations to have a negative impact on self-esteem. Here are ways you can restate your own evidence before it has a negative impact.

Match and Reflect

Every time you create evidence about yourself, match it to your best and highest core values and beliefs. If one of your core beliefs is, "I am a caring person who delivers value to other people," reinforce each and every shred of evidence you find that actually supports that core belief. When you encounter a situation where you have satisfied a customer, or made your kids happy with a special day or treat, think to yourself, "That's just like me!" When you miss the mark, don't kick yourself around the block—think, "That's not like me," figure out what you should have done, make a silent promise to do it better next time, and move on. When you're challenged with negative thoughts or tempted to read available evidence in an unproductive direction, ask yourself, "Does this thinking match who I am and what I believe in? Will acting on this line of thinking reflect my ideas accurately to others?"

Think about the consequences of confirming negative evidence. What will be the short- and long-term impact of validating evidence that fails to positively affect your self-esteem? How, precisely, will it affect your personal life, your professional life, and your recreational opportunities?

❀ Note: Accurately evaluating the consequences of negative evidence about yourself can be tricky, and will probably require constant practice. Sometimes we are simply unaware of the consequence because we lack past experience. Sometimes our habits kick in and blind us to any potentially negative consequences of thinking about ourselves in a certain way. Sometimes we overlook potential negative consequences, because some past action we associate with self-evaluation resulted in pain, loss, failure, and rejection. Our memory could fail us; even though we may have experienced similar situations that should have pointed us toward positive evidence. We may simply forget what they were. Only constant practice in evaluating your own evidence will help overcome these hurdles.

Connect with a Close Friend

If you need reinforcement for your evidence, ask a trusted friend who shares strong values in areas that mean a great deal to you. Be careful! You must choose your confidant wisely, and make your choice based on long-term relationships. Too often, people open themselves up to the wrong "friends"—people who have very low self-esteem themselves, and who are more than willing to drag us down a notch or two.

And that brings us right back to...

Tiffany's Choice

Remember Tiffany, the student who cut class and had to pay big-time? Although she acted to help a "friend," her choice to skip class compromised at least two core values: honesty and integrity. She also fell short of her own expectations by losing the class presidency and by missing several days of class work, which could lower her straight-A grades. The big question, though, is how she will react to her new situation—whether she will use the experience to repair the problems to her first two pillars, or whether she will tumble down. This is where attitude and evidence come in.

Tiffany has a choice.

One Pathway: If Tiffany reacts negatively and decides to rebel, her attitude will propel her self-esteem downward. Suppose she tells herself, "You'd think I was a criminal! All I did was cut class for one day. All my hard work campaigning! And for what? To humiliate me. You'd think I was doing drugs or something. Four weeks without a phone means I can't call my friends, and if I can't call my friends, they'll forget I exist. They'll think I don't want to hang out with them anymore. The teacher, the principal, and my parents have succeeded in making my life miserable!"

Here we have a classic example of negative self-talk. Tiffany's attitude could make a real self-esteem crisis. As the days pass, she could focus less and less on her core values, and become more concerned about losing her "friends." (Sad to say, some of these friends aren't really concerned for Tiffany's long-term welfare.) Say, she walks home with a small group who are just as convinced as Tiffany that the world is out to get them. Someone lights a joint and passes it to Tiffany. Would she accept it? With her characteristics compromised, her expectations low, and her attitude down, Tiffany would be at high risk to justify a very poor choice. "Why not? Everyone is acting like I'm a criminal already. And obviously, I wasn't cut out to be a student government type. What have I got to lose? I might as well enjoy myself some of the time." The low self-esteem snowball has started to roll down the hill, and it's about to pick up speed.

Another Path: Instead of blaming the world (or herself) for the situation, Tiffany might stop, look, and listen—evaluate the situation carefully—and come up with a plan of action to support growing self-esteem. She'd have to recognize that she'd made a mistake by cutting class (especially since she was in a leadership position in school), and she'd have to make an effort to repair the key characteristics that support her positive growth. She'd also have to find some way to upgrade her attitude (and her social circle), and she'd have to see the overall process as part of a learning experience.

She might tell herself something like this: "I went through the pain of losing the class presidency so that I could build up the strength I'd need to face other challenges. I made a mistake, and I thought I was doing the right thing, but I've learned from the experience... and I've now got enough time on my hands to concentrate on making the honor roll this semester."

Is it always easy to pick the second path, rather than the first? No! Building up positive self-esteem is a lifetime task filled with a thousand opportunities for setbacks and improvement. Only practice and commitment will help develop the instincts to avoid picking the "downward slope" of negative self-talk that results in lower self-esteem. Only practice and commitment will help you make a conscious choice to select more constructive forms of internal expression.

Which Will It Be?

"What an idiot! I must be losing my mind. I locked my keys in the car and left the lights on!"

"Look at that. I got distracted because I was preoccupied with that big presentation. Next time, I'll remember to take the car keys—but for now, while I'm waiting for the Triple-A truck, I'll have time to go over my strategy for the big meeting tomorrow one more time."

"Oh, no! I've disappointed my daughter again! I waited too long to order the tickets to the Ice Capades. She'll never forgive me... I'm a terrible parent."

"Oh no! I forgot to get the tickets for the Ice Capades! I'll have to think of a way to turn this into something special... I've got it! Sally and I will catch the show in a different city. We'll make a weekend of it. This will be good for both of us: we'll get quality time and plenty of relaxation."

Monitor yourself for a day—and make it your goal to turn every negative message into a positive, self-esteem building message.

Taking Stock

Do you understand the stock market? Boy, sometimes I don't. How could the price of a company's stock increase—when its balance sheet shows a net value of "zero" at the end of a year? I was up all night last night wondering about that one.

Wait a minute. Perhaps the value of the company is based on something other than simple profit and loss numbers. I'm thinking of things like reputation, image, ethics, policies and procedures, future direction, and how a company takes care of (and invests in) its own employees and customers. Perhaps the value of the company rests on its guiding principles, values, and capabilities.

Now, I'm thinking out loud here, but I'll bet that's what drives stock values up in these situations. I'll bet that's why big-time investors look at all aspects of a company, not just the "hard numbers," before investing large sums of money.

Hey, I've got an idea! I'm going to create a new company called Me, Incorporated. Oh, I won't trade it on the stock market, but I will increase my value—my self-esteem—each and every day. I know that my internal value, my positive sense of self, doesn't include everything within my "firm," but I also know that the my company can deliver nothing of value without it.

I'll continue to learn and develop positive new convictions, and live in accordance with constructive core values. By doing so, I'll increase the internal value that makes all other value-deliveries possible and I'll demolish the competition! I'll be on the cover of every small business magazine in the country! All the experts will want to know how I pulled off such a miracle! Only you and I will know.

~ *Chapter 8* ~

Unstoppability

What is unstoppability? It's the purpose, resolve, and consciousness that makes you be who you want to be and do what you want to do—no matter what stands in your way. To build your own unstoppability, you must ask yourself difficult questions: What stands in the way of achievement? What stops you in your tracks? What makes you say to yourself, "Never mind the obstacle, this is worth it." How many "work-arounds" will you try before giving up?

In this chapter, I want to show you how to develop the essential skills to help you become truly unstoppable.

Everyone Is Unstoppable... at First!

It seems that we're used to thinking of unstoppability—that is, the successful implementation of a "won't take no for an answer" philosophy—as something quite rare. This is not the case. Virtually every person you've met—whether overachiever, underachiever, or non-achiever—once had a relentless drive, a passion for experience, learning, and accomplishment that would not be denied!

If you don't believe me, track down the nearest baby and watch as he or she masters the art of walking.

Drew's Story

Not long ago, I had the honor of watching human unstoppability in action. The human in question was a sweet toddler named Drew; he was surrounded by parents and other relatives hoping to offer support and encouragement as he tried to take a real, honest-to-goodness step. His focus and dedication to his goal was truly remarkable. So was the support he received.

"Come on, Drew, you can to it!" His dad smiled like a benevolent giant. Drew took his hand, stood up slowly, extended an unsteady foot, and collapsed in a heap. Then came the beautiful part.

For the 14th time, Drew got up and tried again.

"Here, Drew, let me help you." Drew's mother took his hand and tried to steady him. The uncertain foot shot forward, and again little Drew tumbled to the floor.

How many times would he fall over during a given week? Hundreds, perhaps thousands. How many bumps and bruises would he suffer? More than any of us in the room cared to imagine. How many times would he cry after falling? Plenty. On one or two occasions, his parents would no doubt feel like crying, too. But more often, they would find a reason to enjoy when Drew's efforts to get his legs to do what he knew, deep down inside, what they were made to do.

For half an hour, I watched as he fell just a little short of his goal—over and over and over again. I watched one of the most inspiring elements of the human spirit, a tenacity we somehow unlearn over the years, but which is, and always has been, our birthright: the right to try again after we "fail."

Drew simply would not quit, even when fatigue got the better of him and the goal of walking would have to be pursued again tomorrow. You could tell he knew that he was on to something. There was no question in his mind: this walking business was going to become second nature to him, somehow, some way, and bumps and bruises were not going to stop him from attaining that goal.

Sure enough, a week or so after I watched him struggle—and fail—to take that momentous First Step, Drew was walking from point to point with all the dizzy overconfidence of a teenager who's just been awarded his driving permit. "Walk? Do I know how to walk? Sure, I know how to walk! Watch this!" That's what he seemed to say as he showed off three gleeful steps before he found himself earthbound again. He'd only narrowly missed the corner of a table with his forehead. But he was walking.

To be fair, all Drew had really learned was how to expose himself to another round of (potentially more serious) bumps and bruises. The same can be said of just about any rewarding activity! There is always some risk involved when it comes to opening up to growth. But Drew, I think, had the advantage over most of us. He still felt, deep down in his gut, that there was no alternative to doing what had to be done. He hadn't learned—he hadn't yet been taught—to hold back or quit.

Eyes on the Prize!

Why is it that children will try over and over to learn how to walk? They will push forward, no matter what. They simply refuse to give up. They never, ever let "failures" distract them. They keep their "eyes on the prize"—the goal of walking from one spot in the house to another. In pursuit of that goal, they will try just about everything: leaning forward, leaning backward, flailing their arms, falling on their hands, falling on their rumps, leaning on a nearby coffee table, or gaining momentum by pushing themselves from a nearby grownup's knee. You name it, and they'll try it. They become resourceful, creative, and fixated on their goal. They try from every angle. And they get lots of encouragement from the adult world in the process!

Then something strange happens. The adult world finds reasons to criticize that once-prized creativity and persistence. In the process, the grownup world starts to teach us to lose sight of that "no matter what" mindset.

Recently, I visited Drew and I noticed two very big changes. For one thing, he was now a really great walker. It appeared to me at times that he was close to breaking the land speed record for the "Transit-living room" event in the upcoming Summer Olympics!

The second thing I noticed was that the voices of family members, who had once been so supportive of his every move and new strategy, now took a very different tone. "Don't do that..." "Stop that or you'll get hurt..." "If I see you doing that one more time, you'll go straight to your room!"

That's how the cycle begins. We want to protect, teach, and guide, but we sometimes limit spirits in the process, cutting back on an individual's ability to enter that "unstoppable" frame of mind. Yes, it is important to learn right from wrong, and yes, someone must watch over children who grow up in a world of danger and pitfalls. But too often, we also encourage our children to unlearn the extraordinary skill of developing tenacious beliefs about their own capacity of achievement. Maybe that's why so few adults retain this remarkable ability.

Once they grow up, children need to muster the resolve and purpose to attain their dreams. They need to learn the art of supporting themselves mentally—telling themselves "I *can* do that!"—because, in the outside world, they will find far more naysayers then yeasayers.

"No Matter What!"

To develop true unstoppability—a prerequisite for taking full advantage of the Power of Will—we must reclaim that glorious "no matter what" mindset. (I've known more than one successful entrepreneur who was described as "childlike" in this regard.)

We must find a way around obstacles and challenges that stop our dreams and goals. We must take a hint from Drew. We must accept that our mission cannot be put on hold, and that we must evaluate every effort in a given area according to a single standard: Will this effort make the attainment of my desire more or less likely?

We must recruit, cajole, and convince others who can help us make our goal a reality. We must collect enough strategies, and enough allies, to win what we're after... somehow... no matter what!

I can think of many phrases to describe this way of thinking, but "unstoppability" is about as close as I can come to combining them into a single word. What we are really talking about here is the "eye of the tiger"—a special kind of single-minded, goal-oriented focus and awareness. This mindset is not obsession or tunnel vision; it is far more creative and adaptive, much closer to a wide-angle view. To be truly unstoppable, you must be willing to try anything and everything that will get you closer to the selected goals.

Four Characteristics

I believe there are four major characteristics simultaneously present in people who make a habit of building unstoppability into their lives. Like Drew, these people are:

- Flexible. (Drew tried lots of different approaches.)
- Courageous. (Drew kept going even though there was the risk of getting hurt.)
- Persistent. (Drew did not stop trying, even when confronted with "failure" in every early approach.)
- Persuasive. (Drew's belief in his goal helped him establish rapport with a supportive group who helped him attain it.)

Flexibility

Have you ever personally witnessed hurricane damage?

I have. The epic storm in question hit a tiny Caribbean island where my wife and I were vacationing. The greatest fury was in the early morning hours. When I went out from the relative safety of our hotel room to survey the damage, I realized that I was lucky to be alive.

The winds had tossed huge yachts around like toy boats. It tore the roofs off of large buildings. It pulverized the concrete piers where cruise ships had offloaded hundreds of happy tourists a few days before. It destroyed homes and killed wildlife and left more than one hapless human being wondering whether he'd picked the right vacation spot. This island, I thought, would take 10 years to rebuild.

And then, as I scanned the landscape, I saw the most amazing thing. Actually, I saw a whole slew of amazing things! In the middle of this destruction, there was clear evidence that not everything on this unlucky island would have to be rebuilt, replanted, or relocated.

Not a single palm tree had been blown down. Not one.

They were in perfect condition, as though winds of 120 miles per hour had never blown through them, as though waves of 20 to 30 feet hadn't pounded the shores for hours on end, as though nothing had happened at all. Every palm tree still stood tall and beautiful after enduring the wind and the waves.

Why? Because they knew how to bend! Nearly everything that had tried to face those ferocious winds—everything that had been built to stay rigid and fixed in a single position—had taken a beating. But the palm trees were supple enough to give way and blow to one side or another without becoming uprooted. That's a valuable skill!

Being unstoppable is *not* the same as being unyielding. Rigidly committing to every single one of the "demands" that will get you to your goal is a great way to antagonize other people.

People who "don't budge" when evaluating their tactics have a way of unleashing storms of harshness and egotism in themselves—and in others! The trick is to know when to retreat, when to go with the flow, when to give a little, and when to make an effort to learn the different ways to work toward your goal. When Drew committed himself to learning how to walk, he didn't pick only one starting point, and he didn't use only one learning routine. He took what was in front of him and tried to learn from it. He showed flexibility.

People who are unstoppable in the most constructive and life-affirming sense know that taking a headstrong, stubborn, or abusive attitude toward the world or people they interact with is always a losing proposition. They are out to win for themselves *and other people*, and they know that sometimes they will have to bend a little in one area in order to make progress in another. A river can't be stopped—but it may come up against a really big rock. That's no problem. It just goes around the rock!

Why do so many people mistake being a diehard for unstoppability? I think part of the problem is our fixation with sports metaphors. In our culture, the idea of one person or entity "winning" is often strongly connected with another person's "losing." Actually, many other outcomes benefit everyone involved.

There is such a thing as a "multilateral" win—and people who take full advantage of the Power of Will know it. They don't get taken in by the empty talk of "being number one" or "second place is the first loser." They know that any comparison that uses a scoreboard with a clear winner and loser, or pits one side against another, or contrasts a "favorite" with an "underdog," is a *limited* image. It leads to a rigid, inflexible mindset. Off the court or the field, life is a little more complicated. There are ways to "win" that don't involve humiliating or manipulating others, or making anyone feel like a "loser." Any truly professional salesperson can tell you that!

~

If you're doing anything other than actually engaging in a sport that uses a scoreboard, fixating on "beating the other side" will lead to rigid, inflexible patterns of behavior that will hurt your cause.

~

Set egos aside, and focus on multilateral wins! Granted, this is easier said than done, but no matter what your gender, your goal, or your personality style, you can find a way to use your ego—your viewpoint, the power of your persuasion—in a constructive, positive way that benefits everyone. (Yes, that even applies to Driver personalities!) The trick is to put your ego, which is a source of considerable strength, to work pursuing goals that benefit everyone.

Business relationships and personal relationships both *need* people with egos. Without ego involvement, there's no drive or movement. But these relationships also need people who can keep ego concerns in perspective—people who can laugh at themselves, people who can put relationships with others first, and people who know that "victory" is different from always getting your own way.

In short, any good relationship needs people who are willing to serve each other's needs. In virtually every important relationship, this means "winning" by finding a way to help someone else attain a key objective—not by finding reasons to label someone else a "loser."

Put your ego to work serving others. They'll return the favor!

Here's a list of ways to increase your flexibility and open yourself up to new ideas and new ways to accomplish goals that benefit you *and* other people. Use them to build up your "try this instead" muscle!

⚘ Take into account the feelings and opinions of other people. This is the big one—the skill most adults need to compensate for their natural, toddler-vintage creativity and adaptability that is often stifled by the outside world! Yes, I know. You've heard advice about "playing well with others" before, and it's often easier to discuss this idea than to practice it. All the same, considering other people really is the first step toward building greater flexibility in your personal or professional life. Practice exploring the emotional implications an action will have on the other people in your life. Before you make a decision affecting people you love, ask family members about their preferences. At work, solicit opinions from other team members;

don't just "announce the plan." Once you engage people in the decision making process, you'll find they rate your ideas with greater enthusiasm and conviction—and share key information, too.

❀ Screen your messages. No, I'm not talking about turning on your telephone answering machine. I'm talking about thinking before you speak, about getting a "second opinion" about that letter you're planning to send out to team members who ticked you off. Does what you say really convey the message and your meaning? Is that letter harsher than you intended? Negatively charged words and phrases will always turn people off—and they'll usually deprive you of the needed critical feedback when it's time to change direction! Before you say or write anything important to someone else, play it back inside your head. Say it to *yourself* first and ask yourself, "How would I receive this message if I had the other person's position and viewpoint?"

❀ Look for the second best idea. If you want to become more flexible and adopt a greater feeling of creativity in your work and in life, then develop the habit of looking beyond the obvious. Don't settle for the first answer (whether it's yours or someone else's). Explore new alternatives and possibilities. Maybe what seems to be your best option should really be your backup plan!

❀ Learn a new skill or find a new technology you can use every day. Learning has a wonderful way of neutralizing the human ego while increasing flexibility! If you've always left the cooking to your spouse or partner, why not take his or her out-of-town business trip as an opportunity to actually cook something, rather than heat prepared meals in the microwave? If you spend a lot of time at your word processor, experiment with one of the voice-recognition text development programs. If your Day Timer is always a mess, think about purchasing a Palm Pilot or other personal electronic/computerized organizer. Don't make the mistake of *constantly* attempting to "implement" new technological advances, but be prepared, once every other month or so, to take a look around and "see what's out there." Don't do this to "keep up with the Joneses"—do it to keep up with the times! New skills keep you from thinking you know it all (none of us do). New technology helps you make sense of the world in new ways, while getting more done!

❀ Volunteer to teach. Anyone who's ever led a Cub Scout den can testify that teaching can be a humbling experience, one that leaves the instructor far wiser than he or she was before. If you need to remind yourself that people process information at varying speeds and with varying attention levels, gather a group of eight-year-olds and try to engage them on a single topic for 60 minutes! People can (and will) interpret your messages in different ways; people can (and will) want to ask questions that you hadn't anticipated. Assuming that you're not taking the blunt, dictatorial, "my way or the highway" approach (and you certainly shouldn't), you'll find that effectively teaching students of any age is a great way to learn and practice the value of flexibility. Pick a familiar subject—basketball, soccer, basic accounting—and then share what you know!

❀ Go out of your way to experience new and different things during leisure time. Turn off the television and surf the Net to find out about a different country—and consider making that site your next vacation spot. Or visit a new restaurant, one that features food prepared in a way you've never tasted. Or attend festivals or plays that depict a different culture or historical period. Or try to learn a new language. (Don't worry about becoming fluent—the aim is to discover the essentials of communicating in a way that's presently unfamiliar to you.) Consciously seeking change and new experience in pleasurable settings automatically sends important messages to your brain: Adapting to new situations is fun! Send that message often.

Then, when a circumstance related to a key goal arises that requires flexibility, your subconscious will kick in and look for innovative new ways to make your goal a reality. The deepest recesses of your brain will work as an ally, not an enemy, when you need to set a new course toward your goal.

How committed are you to developing flexibility in your life? The answer to that question depends on your desire to grow and prosper continually by reinforcing this key component of unstoppability.

In life, the temptation to become set in our ways can become amazingly strong. We have to fight that temptation. We have to sway like the palm tree, so we don't get flattened during one of life's many storms!

Courage

The dictionary defines "courage" as "the ability to face danger, difficulty, threats, or physical pain without fear." I think that definition is a little misleading. I prefer the more pragmatic version circulated among the cowboys of the American West: "Courage is being scared, but saddling up anyway."

The number of movies, books, and songs celebrating supposedly "fearless" people is mind-boggling and has created a cult of worship that has led many to believe that "fearlessness" is a necessary quality. Actually, the person who operates without fear is what I call "stupid."

Fear plays a very important role for us; it alerts us to potential danger or trauma, and helps us avoid past situations with bad endings. The trick is to control fear, to put it in its place, and to learn from it when appropriate—not to try to eradicate it entirely, which is an unrealistic goal.

In my opinion, understanding fear is a far better idea than eliminating fear. When I think back, I realize that times when I felt totally "fearless," I exposed myself needlessly to significant dangers. I had no idea that peril and disappointment lay just ahead, and in many cases, I got knocked around as a result. A little fear would have been a real blessing!

Understand that I'm not talking about living a life that's ruled by fear, but about effectively interpreting the messages fear sends our way. Sometimes a fear can be valid—such as when you realize that someone who's repeatedly let you down in the past is in a position to do so again. Understand the basis of that fear, then act on it appropriately and move on to something else. At other times, a particular fear does not warrant a great deal of attention. Let's say you hold back on developing a new skill, for fear that you'll make a fool of yourself the first time you try to use that skill. A realistic analysis of this fear will lead to the conclusion that it's a major "disabler"—something that blocks growth and keeps you from living the life you deserve. In each case, *examining* the fear—rather than intensifying it instinctively—is the first step toward determining whether it points toward something you need to address.

～

Ignoring fears can be fatal; letting fears run your life can be fatal, too.

～

There are four levels of competency or awareness that help us understand and quantify fears related to each situation we encounter. These awareness levels play an important part in building what I call "real courage"—courage that's rooted in understanding, not foolhardiness. This courage makes unstoppability a reality! Take a look at the four awareness levels now.

1　Conscious competence. This is the highest level of awareness. You apply all of your abilities to the situation at hand.

2　Unconscious competence. This is a step closer to danger. You're unaware of why you're able to do whatever it is you're doing; you're on autopilot. You're not consciously thinking about what's happening, or of any future consequences.

3   Conscious incompetence. This is the best place to be
       when learning new skills and abilities. You're aware that
       you don't know something you need to know, and you
       work to raise your competency level in a given area. If you
       respond intelligently to a situation of conscious incompe-
       tence, you'll realize that there are areas where it's best to
       proceed with caution—or not proceed at all until you
       build your skills.

4   Unconscious incompetence. This is the lowest level of
       awareness, and the point where danger is at the highest
       level. You don't know what you don't know. Improvement
       and awareness in a given area is unlikely until you realize
       there's a problem. Until that time, you're either "clueless"
       or "fearless"—I'll leave the choice of terminology up to you.

When it comes to making unstoppability a reality, the true
courage is *knowledge*—having the skills necessary to deliver
precisely the results you need in a particular situation. That
understanding matches up with the top level in the four-part
analysis above, that of the consciously competent person.

In that scenario, you've got a *reason* to be courageous. You're
operating at peak performance, with a significant knowledge
base, and you can forecast the likely outcome of your actions.
You use the historical information—but you don't let it paralyze
or limit your potential achievement.

~

Knowledge is the proper response to fear—not denial!

~

To move yourself into the conscious competency level, ask
yourself the following questions.

§   While I'm performing at my very best in a particular
    area, am I still looking for ways to improve?

§   After I've completed a task, do I still take time to practice
    key skills to get even better?

§ Do I perform "post-mortems"—post-project analyses that help identify what worked (and what didn't)?

§ When I "fail" to do my very best, do I make a point of asking "Why?"

§ Do I take constructive criticism well?

§ Am I committed to finding a way to increase my level of performance, even after a significant success?

§ Do I avoid, at all costs, taking a "know-it-all" attitude?

§ Do I keep an eye out for new resources to help me improve in all areas?

Beware—a single "no" answer to any of the above questions means you're riding for a fall. Commit yourself to developing real courage—the kind that reflects the mindset of someone at the top of their game and always looking to improve. Build up your own skills and aptitudes!

Persistence

Persistence, as we've seen, does not mean inflexibility. Persistence simply means coming back, again and again, to the task of attaining one's goal.

Persistence means harnessing a motivating force that was in our brain *before we had the words with which to choose it*. How about that? In order to master the complexities of language, of motor coordination, of walking (as Drew's story indicates), or any of a thousand other activities, we have to do something special. We must be able to take advantage of an *inborn* ability to return, time after time after time, to the most important question we will ever contemplate: "What else would work?" We ask ourselves this question before we know how to talk!

We must learn to become resourceful, learn to look at problems as opportunities, and learn to *monitor our progress toward our goals* and change what doesn't work. Pilots who fly those big jet airliners have to set a flight plan—but they also have to keep an eye on the autopilot! This is a little machine that automatically makes course corrections every three or four seconds, because the plane spends most of its time off course by a small amount!

~

The key to persistence is not to keep doing what doesn't work, but to make corrections quickly and accurately, and to avoid "overcorrections" that would make the situation worse.

~

I've already dealt with persistence as a cornerstone of unstoppability earlier in this chapter. Let me emphasize that there's a big difference between being persistent and being a pest. To me, the distinction lies in one's creativity and enthusiasm.

A persistent person tries all possible angles, and thinks up a few new ones for good measure, in working to overcome objections, obstacles, and doubt. By contrast, a pest rarely brings anything new to the situation! He or she simply makes the same calls, asks the same questions, and applies the same annoying strategies, without ever monitoring what's working and what isn't.

Persistent people inspire confidence; they seem to have an internal equanimity, a peace of mind that lets others know that everything's going to be all right. Pests act as though the world were always about to end. They're big on crises.

Persistence is akin to loyalty; it builds up relationships. "Pestiness" is based on mistrust; it's always focused on short-term outcomes and usually signifies a low degree of confidence in the other person's good will and sense of fair play.

Persistent people believe in themselves and their cause. They constantly ask the magic question—"What else would work?"—because they truly believe in what they're doing. Pests often give every indication that they expect others to do the believing (and the implementing) for them.

The bottom line: Persistent people are internally secure enough to experiment—and pests are so internally insecure that they constantly require initiative, validation, approval, or action from others!

Persistence goes hand in hand with the fourth element of unstoppability...

Persuasiveness

A major component of unstoppability is one's ability to influence others, to get them to take action on behalf of the goal.

If you're going to attain goals that require assistance, you need to learn how to build alliances, how to affect them in a positive way, and how to get them to leave a conversation nodding their heads and saying to themselves, "You know, that person's got a point." In short, you need to figure out how to persuade people.

Persuasion is an art, not a science. Contrary to what you may have heard or read, it does *not* consist of simply "mirroring" the speech patterns, breathing rate, colloquialisms, or posture of the person with whom you're interacting. It's more complex.

As someone who has been "mirrored" more times than I care to recall, I can attest that it's an irritating and insulting process that most individuals recognize and resent instantly. In a business or personal setting, more people will be turned off than impressed by this approach.

I realize that this observation runs counter to the advice of many "experts"—but I call them as I see them, friends. For anyone building meaningful relationships on a regular basis, "mirroring" is a bankrupt interpersonal strategy. It doesn't build bridges; it only irritates or confuses the person you're trying to connect with.

This "mirroring" strategy goes by a lot of other names—modeling, pacing, feeding back the other person's input, and so on. Beyond the (common-sense) notion that any person is likely to be most comfortable when he or she is controlling the sequence and pace of a given conversation, there really isn't anything of value in any of these strategies. Ignore them!

There is potential for some (unintentional) comedy in the "mirroring" philosophy. I've always wondered what would happen when two people tried to use it on each other at the same time, not realizing that each was attempting to reflect the other's movements, vocal pitch, breathing, and so on! I'd love to be there when it happens.

Personal Rapport, Business Rapport

The art of persuasion falls into two basic categories: personal rapport and business rapport. Although there is some overlap in the two areas—some people will be true friends and important business acquaintances—the motives involved in the two kinds of rapport-building are fundamentally different.

When we're aiming to build personal rapport with someone, we're establishing a connection based on mutual understanding and appreciation of that person's opinions, hobbies, feelings, emotions, culture, past experience, or present situation. In a business situation, we're establishing a relationship in which what needs to be done is being done the best way possible. In this setting, personal experience, values, feelings, and all the rest are fine—but they're not as important as the business objective we share with the person in question.

Master the art of building personal rapport, and you'll enjoy persuasiveness that leads to better relationships, expanding influence, and greater satisfaction and fulfillment. Master the art of building business rapport, and you'll enjoy persuasiveness that leads to long-term career success, important mentor relationships, and significant financial rewards.

When you build personal rapport, you increase the number of people who could call you in the middle of the night with good (or bad) news. When you build business rapport, you increase the number of people who want you to help them build skyscrapers where two-story buildings once existed.

Building Personal Rapport

Rapport—of either variety—takes time to build. It's not an instant process, or a succession of simple steps you take within the first 10 minutes of a new acquaintance. You may run into someone with whom you "click" more or less instantly, because of shared common experiences. But that's pretty rare.

Let's look at the common pitfalls—what you should definitely avoid while building the personal rapport that will help you be persuasive at the social level (other than "mirroring").

❀ Being late. Talk about a great way to make a lousy first (or second, or third) impression! Outside of dying, I can't think of a single event where being late is to your advantage. Do things come up from time to time that keep us from maintaining time commitments? Sure. But when they do, it sends an unmistakable message that we place little or no value on the other person's time. Complete your obligations ahead of time!

❀ Procrastination of any kind. A variation on the "being late" theme, procrastination in a social situation occurs when you fail to deliver on a promise, whether or not there's a clear time slot involved. ("I meant to bring you that article you asked for—I'll try to remember it next time.") Procrastinating sends a clear signal to the other party that you have let some other activity (or no activity at all) take precedence over commitments.

❀ Talking down other people or things. Have you ever been cornered by a "complainer"—someone who basically lived to find fault with people, institutions, and all of our Maker's creations? Did the ranting make you want to engage that person on a long-term basis? Not long ago I found myself trapped in the back seat of a New York City cab. The driver used our (45-minute!) ride to the airport as an excuse to tell me what he didn't like about the city, his job, family, the economy, our country... I've never been so happy to be inside an air terminal in all my life! Don't run even the slightest risk of being mistaken for a complainer. Follow my mother's oft-repeated rule: "If you can't say something nice, don't say anything at all." (Thanks, mom. You're an angel.)

✼ Pretending to know someone or something you don't. It can be very tempting to mislead another person about your status, connectedness, income, level of expertise, whatever. Don't do it for two big reasons. First, lying is complex and wrong. It's hard work to keep everything straight! Later on in the relationship, the person may appeal to something you've said as though you were telling the gospel truth—and, whether you mean to or not, you'll have that weird look in your eye: "I said what?" Second reason: we live in a small world these days! That story about saving three or four dozen people during the latest Midwestern flood may haunt you when your new friend does a little searching on the Internet, or connects with an old colleague who knows you've never set foot west of the Hudson River.

✼ Asking for a favor before you've earned the right. Greed and opportunism are never pretty, but at the outset of any relationship, they're particularly off-putting. The best outcome is to make the other person feel comfortable enough in your friendship to come to you for help. Parinello's All-Purpose Definition of "Personal Rapport" is worth remembering here—and elsewhere.

~

Rapport: Making the other person feel more comfortable, special, and more important than you.

~

So much for the *don'ts*—what *should* you do to build personal rapport?

✼ Listen with extreme interest and empathy. I've spoken at length about the importance of developing excellent listening skills in other aspects of life. These skills are particularly important when building your powers of persuasion in the personal realm. There's another suggestion that may interest you in social (and, yes, business) settings. Use supportive verbal statements ("Oh, really?" "Is that right?" "How interesting!" etc.) at appropriate points in the dialogue. This builds up the other person's "comfort level" quickly and effectively.

❀ Show sincere interest in the other person. Be more concerned about being an interested person than about being an interesting one. Here, as in so many areas where establishing persuasiveness and building rapport are the goals, the rule of reciprocity is all-important. If you take the first step and show your interest in the other person, then that person will in turn show interest in you. (Keep reading for some more examples of this principle!)

❀ Shock the person by doing something nice for no apparent reason. If you're looking for a great way to build instant rapport with someone you don't yet know, this is hard to beat. Say a new person is starting at the office today. Even though you're busy putting the final touches on your sales forecast—you've got a big meeting with the boss tomorrow morning—you take five minutes to prepare a signed WELCOME poster and leave it on the new person's desk. Bingo! You've taken the first all-important step in building a friend—and a potential ally—for life!

❀ Find out what matters to the other person, then make it the focus of the conversation. At the outset of the conversation, stick with open-ended questions or brief stories from someone else's past. This will encourage the other person to open up. Avoid overwhelming your new acquaintance with tasteless jokes, endless monologues, or details from your personal life that he or she may view as inappropriate.

❀ Be easy to approach. How, you ask? Come on. You already know how. Make initial, non-threatening eye contact. Smile. Focus with full attention. Be courteous at all times.

If you use these tools to build and maintain personal rapport, you'll have a much easier time building relationships (and persuading people of the merits of your viewpoint) than you will if you "steamroll" them with endless words and opportunistic hand-pumping.

Building Business Rapport

Whenever your aim is to build business rapport, you must act as though you're on a job interview because you are!

The list of *don'ts* for building business rapport starts out with some familiar entries. Just like in a personal setting, you must avoid at all costs:

- ❀ Showing up late for anything (or otherwise mismanaging your time). This is, if anything, an even more important principle in business. Find a way to make the meeting! Find a way to complete your obligations ahead of time! If you can help someone achieve a goal (or, better yet, over-achieve a goal) *and* you can complete the work early, you'll be a star forever in that person's eyes.

- ❀ Procrastinating. A sound business relationship demands that the people involved do what they say they'll do, when they said they'd do it. Period.

- ❀ Engaging in negative talk about anyone or anything. Who has time for whiners or people who broadcast nasty rumors?

- ❀ Pretending to know someone or something you don't. Remember, key players within a given industry usually know one another!

- ❀ Asking for a favor before you've earned the right. This is a particularly grievous mistake when you're dealing with someone of greater influence and authority.

- ❀ "Breaking the ice." In some cultures, elaborate and lengthy social conversational rituals must precede any business discussion. Guess what? The United States of America is not one of those cultures! For decades, doz-ens—no, hundreds—of self-appointed business experts have been telling salespeople and others to use a little "small talk" to reduce tension, improve the atmosphere, and get things off to a smooth start at the beginning of a meeting. It doesn't work! In 26 years of professional selling, this "breaking the ice" technique has never improved the discussion for me. Not once! At this point in my career, I've heard enough horror stories about this technique to shy away from it completely, and I suggest that you do the same. Case in point: Robert Coates, a fellow speaker and author, told me of the time he was escorted into an office to meet a top executive of a large corporation. As he walked in, Robert scanned the office for material he could use to "break the ice." He found something: a photo on the desk. As he shook hands with his contact, Robert said, "It looks like your son's Little League team sure is doing well." The executive's reply? It was brisk: "This isn't my office, Mr. Coates. Now, what was it you were here to see me about?" Ouch!

❀ Overstating or under-delivering anything. Business rapport is based on trust, and trust comes when we set expectations and then meet (or preferably, exceed) those expectations. Sure—sometimes you fail to hit a business goal. But it's never okay to set up a false expectation by making inflated or exaggerated statements and then under-deliver.

⌒

It's impossible to make up for a lack of knowledge or experience with a mastery of people skills!

⌒

❀ Criticizing anyone's efforts. This is especially important when you're talking about something currently being used by your contact. Years ago, at the end of a four-hour tour of a facility, a VP asked me whether I had questions. "Just one," I said. "How long have you had that disorganized and confusing maze of terminal cabling in your data center?" The answer came back so quickly that it literally left me speechless: "Since my son designed and installed it five years ago!" (I didn't get the business.)

❀ Tell trade secrets or share confidential or privileged information. This one should be a no-brainer, but people constantly forget the importance of showing professional discretion in business settings. Think it through. If you show or say something that you aren't supposed to, how will your contact know you won't breach confidences again when you're talking to his or her competitors?

❀ Assuming that business rapport will carry over into personal rapport. Though a person may do business with you, this doesn't mean he or she will invite you to a family event. Attempting to treat business acquaintances as personal acquaintances can lead to the perception that you're "taking liberties"—especially early in the relationship. People may enjoy a business relationship with you, and conduct their personal life in a very different (and very private) sphere. That's not right or wrong—it's something you must honor.

Those are pitfalls you must avoid in building business rapport and positioning yourself as a persuasive, polished professional. What's on the positive side? What do you need to do? Here are some suggestions.

❀ Gain favorable attention in an appropriate way early in the relationship. Yes, this boils down to "making a positive first impression"—but in a business setting, you must be sure your "first impression" includes what the person hears, sees, and feels during the first *and last* few seconds of any meeting. Your "entrance" and "exit" are critical to the development of business rapport in the early going. You must know questions you'll ask to gain interest and attention in the early going. To end on a high note, you may want to preview a future question about the person's career or recent accomplishments: "The next time we talk, I'd love for you to tell me what your greatest challenges were when you..." To the degree that you can, plan your entrance *and* exit carefully.

❀ Consistently exceed expectations. The fastest way to build credibility—a key component of persuasiveness—is to do what you say you will, or more. Make sure it gets done—and then some! If you can, set up a system of self-reward (financial or otherwise), so your brain gets the message that good things happen when you go the extra mile for people.

⁓

In order to succeed, you must exceed!

⁓

❀ Make yourself an appreciating asset. Deliver increasing levels of *real* and *perceived* value over time. Continue to bring new ideas, greater information, and enhanced levels of service to your contact's business. Do what nobody else does. Live with these challenges! Be sure you're viewed as an *indispensable* contributor. When the time comes to reorganize the company, you want to be on the list of people who offer something unique and irreplaceable—not on the list of people whose business appeal can best be summarized as "me, too." You're goal should be to become a partner, not just a vendor or employee or colleague. Partners have influence! Partners have persuasion power!

❀ Demonstrate a commitment to continued improvement. Never give your contact reason to assume that you've become intellectually, emotionally, or physically stagnant. Show your commitment to growth in all areas of life—in particular, keep up with this person's industry. Find out the business authors and topics he or she follows. Read the newest book in this category—one your contact has not read—and then send along a copy for him or her to read. Compose an intelligent handwritten note for the title page. Wham! You've established yourself as someone who's "in the know," someone with a valuable opinion.

❀ Always be upbeat. Everyone appreciates a winning attitude. Everyone enjoys people who handle setbacks and reversals with the right attitude: "Life is good and I am a happy person." Displaying this attitude when stress is high increases the chance this person will call on you for advice during tough times. You want that status! So make the best of each situation during the time you share building rapport with the person. Your mood, attitude, and opinions must be optimistic and uplifting—even if the other person's are not! Remember, attitudes are contagious, so make yours a positive one.

❀ Dress for success. Personal image is an important part of building business rapport. Success really does have a look all its own, which is why I suggest you invest (sensibly) in outfits that make you look and feel like a million bucks. Use the right clothing to inspire higher levels of achievement—not as an empty "uniform" you can hide within.

❀ Be a great team player by instinctively giving credit, rather than instinctively taking it. Every team has room for another unconditional team-first contributor. Let's face it, people have more respect, admiration, and understanding for the "givers" of the world than for the "takers." Shine the spotlight on other team members and contribute without being asked. Display emotional support, a caring and considerate attitude, and generosity of spirit to everyone on this person's team—and talk up those team members (honestly and accurately) when you can.

Business rapport, like personal rapport, takes sustained effort. If you follow the steps I've outlined above, you will, over time, build up business rapport and the ability to persuade and influence key people about the issues that matter most to you. Here, again, the principle of reciprocity holds. Once you act on the issues that matter to them, they'll look for ways to act on issues that matter to you. If they possibly can, they'll support your cause!

CARE

The final word when it comes to building rapport with others is simple. You must always CARE for the individual or organization you have connected with.

C: be *Considerate*.

A: take time to form an *Alliance*.

R: *Relate* to the individual.

E: develop *Equitable* results—make everyone a winner!

What Else Do Unstoppable People Have in Common?

Here are final suggestions to help you develop the purpose, resolve, and focus you need to become unstoppable. The most unstoppable people I've ever met were all:

- Certain of who they were, and in close contact with their own spirituality.
- Ready to look at life as a mission, and are confident in their "higher calling."
- Glowing with radiant positive energy and an optimistic outlook.
- Eager to look for the best in others—and to encourage others to see the best in them.
- Excited about new challenges, and willing to look at them as adventures.
- Capable of putting credit and blame where they belong.
- Responsible and self-controlled.
- Single-minded and flexible; capable of navigating, and seeing beyond distractions.
- Eager to encourage competition.
- Skilled in using frustration, disappointments, and setbacks as energizers.

Unwilling to let disappointment (or anything else) stop them!

Three Little Words

One day, when I was a young boy, my mother washed my mouth out with soap. I think she probably tasted it more than I did. Don't get me wrong—I definitely tasted it! To this day, I can clearly recall the flavor of that bar of Ivory soap.

I'd said a very, very bad word. Not to a school-friend, not to a stranger I passed in the street, but to Vincent, the neighborhood barber. Vincent's was where my dad got his hair cut. For some unfathomable reason, I'd chosen to show off my new, expanded vocabulary during my dad's weekly stop at Vincent's. There'd been a pause in the proceedings after I used this word, a hole in the conversation big enough to accommodate a Mack truck. The minute the word had left my mouth, I had a feeling something terrible was going to happen. The trip home with my father did nothing to dispel that feeling.

My mom thought that if she took action first, my dad would consider the matter settled. He didn't. I had a hard time talking and sitting down for the next few days.

As eavesdropping children, we learn plenty of nasty words. Sometimes we're punished for using them, and eventually we learn enough discretion to understand when such language is inappropriate. But you know what? Prohibiting certain words isn't enough! There are also some words we should definitely encourage our children to say as often as they can. In fact, we should make a point of saying those words ourselves! Why? Because they remind us of the fundamental sources of strength and determination we need in order to become unstoppable. Here are three "F-words" that support unstoppability and build a constructive sense of self-determination. These are words we should celebrate and learn to love in our lives every day, at every opportunity!

§ Friends

§ Family

§ Faith

These deserve constant love, attention and reinforcement. By committing ourselves to loving our friends and family members, and by choosing to strengthen our faith, we can build up significant reserves in our emotional and spiritual "bank accounts." Our long-term investments—our friends, our family, and our faith—can, should, and will support any attempt to build self-determination and unstoppability in life.

∼ Chapter 9 ∼

True Success, True Wealth, and Your Big Goals

How do you define success? How should you identify ultimate destinations in the most important areas of your life? What should you do to establish or fine-tune your key goals?

In this chapter, you'll start putting it all together. You'll learn how success depends on how we choose to classify things and how we react emotionally. You'll find out the true meaning of wealth. (Warning: It's not what most people think!) You'll reestablish a connection with a truly practical understanding of yourself—an understanding you've developed through your work in earlier chapters. You'll also create a complete set of goals that you can use to increase the chances of success (as you define that word) in the areas of your life that matter most.

What Is Success?

Different people have different ideas of what constitutes success. Our choices, our experience, and our daily outlook will affect what we consider to be a supreme positive potential outcome—what we consider to be worth working for (or fighting for), and what we struggle to avoid with all our might—and what qualifies as a dreary "everyday" existence. Consider the following exchange.

"I had the most beautiful dream last night. I was floating through space in a brilliant white space suit. Every inch of my body was sealed up safely."

"Oh, my gosh! Didn't it get claustrophobic, buttoned up inside that suit?"

"No, not at all. I was just floating in space, cut free from the mother ship. I knew I must have gone through the hatch to get to where I was, but the ship was nowhere in sight."

"That's terrifying! Didn't you feel abandoned, marooned?"

"Oh, no, this was the most fascinating sensation: I felt like I could float forever, in any direction. I even woke up wishing that I could find some way to make that dream come true! It may have been the most beautiful dream I've ever had."

"Are you kidding? That sounds like a four-alarm nightmare. I can't even look out a three-story window without getting dizzy!"

On Our Own Terms

I think we are each happiest when defining our terms for success. After all, one person's success may be another's abject failure. Here's another dialogue to ponder.

"Well, they finally gave me the promotion I deserve: vice president of worldwide sales and marketing. I'll be on the fast track, logging those frequent flier miles and meeting the top people in my industry!"

"Lots of travel, huh?"

"A fair amount. I'll only be gone two and a half weeks each month."

"Won't you miss your family?"

"We've talked it over. It will be tough at first, but everyone will adjust, and I think we'll all be a lot happier in the long run. After all, this is a big boost in salary."

"Gee, I wouldn't like the idea of missing out on my kids' soccer games."

"Well, Marge will do my cheering for me. Besides, we'll be able to afford a new minivan and that backyard pool the kids have been lobbying for."

"Yes, but it sounds to me like you may be too busy to enjoy them!"

"You know what? It's more important to me that the kids enjoy that stuff. Besides, this way, I'll get to travel internationally—I've never really gotten to do that, and it's been a major goal of mine for a long time. And now we've got six weeks of vacation a year—so that's going to be some pretty special time for the family, I think. We can all spend a month and a half in Paris together. That will be a blast!"

Defining Success

What does success mean to you? The answers should be your answers—not anyone else's, and certainly not those of the advertising industry!

Many people think of "failure" as the opposite of success, and as something to be avoided. Actually, what is commonly regarded as "failure" is an essential prerequisite to success! The best lessons we ever get are from mistakes! These aren't failures. They're gifts—if we learn from them. "Failing" at something is far better than "succeeding" at nothing through lack of effort.

We do not "fail" until we turn a learning experience into a negative judgment against ourselves. Often, what we choose to identify as "failure" is simply:

§   A lack of focus or purpose—that ability to keep our "eyes on the road" as we head toward a goal we've identified with success.

§ Incomplete or incorrect information—an insistence on moving ahead when we don't have enough facts or necessary data.

§ Lack of drive—the pattern of giving up too early, or failing to examine more creative options.

§ Lack of emotional control—the habit of letting our emotions determine our actions, rather than putting distance between ourselves and the situation.

§ Indecisiveness—the habit of acting too late, or becoming too slow at hitting the switch and allowing a problem to turn into a crisis. This is very different from the habit of taking the time for deliberate fact gathering before making decisions. The ideal decision-making model is to take the time you need to gather facts, and then commit to a decision with full attention and emotional commitment. Such decisions are rarely reversed.

§ Remaining in fear—that is, deciding to let fear dictate our emotional state every time it surfaces. We can't fear temporary setbacks, otherwise we'll find ourselves paralyzed! (My father, a former boxer, used to say, "Don't be afraid of getting knocked down—just make sure you get up one more time than your opponent.")

§ Being overcautious—habitually delaying action until you can be "sure of the outcome." Guess what? There are no guarantees in life! We can never be absolutely sure of a given outcome.

§ Avoiding positive change—that is, clinging to the familiar whether or not it's in our best interests to do so. When the opportunity presents itself for personal growth or progress toward a constructive goal, we must be willing to embrace change.

I believe those are the primary causes of what the world often labels "failure." In each case, we can learn from the experience of encountering obstacles and increase our chances of eventual success. If success is a direction, not a destination—and I believe it is—then the only true "failure" is to give up along the way.

This brings us back to our initial question: What does success mean to you? Where should your journey take you? I think there is only one caveat to define your success:

~

People who define success solely through the amount of money they earn tend to be less happy than people who develop broader definitions.

~

Unfortunately, although that's the only big rule you have to watch out for, it's easy to break in our culture! For years, I've been asking my seminar participants to answer the question, "What does success mean to you?" Judging from the answers, 60 to 70 percent of my alumni see success as being more or less synonymous with having a great deal of money.

It doesn't take much digging to determine the close association between money and success is popular at all levels of our society.

In my experience, although nothing is wrong with establishing motivating financial goals, focusing only on those goals leads to a money obsession that can degenerate into spiritual bankruptcy. I've seen many individuals destroy their lives by fixating on money as all important in their lives. These people exposed themselves to the kind of life-threatening stress of those who make money their first, last, and only quest for success.

I've seen people who achieved their financial goals respond to this "success" by adopting different personalities, unhealthy personal habits, and social images in direct conflict with their most positive values, beliefs, qualities, and traits. I'd personally opt for massive failure!

All too often, people believe that the attainment of financial goals will mean that all the other challenges will simply disappear. Unfortunately, with this money fixation, the opposite occurs. Anxiety, frustration, worry, anger, and a host of other debilitating emotions often accompany large amounts of money.

No, it is not dysfunctional to want to make money and to have possessions. But I believe it is dysfunctional to define success solely in financial terms!

I believe that "wealth" includes, but is not limited to, material riches. If you look in a good dictionary for the word wealth, you'll probably find the words "pleasure," "happiness," "abundance," "well-being," "prosperity," and "health." You won't find any of those words, though, if you look up the definition for "money"!

We can be wealthy in many aspects of our lives. We can only have money in one area: the financial area. To focus only on financial wealth is a little like going to a gymnasium to work out the muscles in your left arm—and ignoring the rest of your body. No matter how magnificent you may be able to get that left arm to look, people are going to wonder why the rest of your physique is underdeveloped!

Total Wealth

Unlike financial riches, this broader idea of multifaceted wealth carries the implication of stability, a sense of continuity and balance. A deeper understanding of wealth brings us in contact with the challenge of developing and enhancing all our internal gifts.

All the money in the world cannot buy the latent wealth within us! We must earn that wealth, and unearth it, by mastering the neglected art of becoming the people we were meant to be.

There are five specific areas of wealth I want to look at in detail:

§ Emotional Wealth

§ Career Wealth

§ Interpersonal Wealth

§ Personal Wealth

§ Financial Wealth

These are not the only beneficial categories. For each of us, there are unique categories of challenges and opportunities that remain dormant until fully expressed. There are hundreds—

probably thousands—of specialized growth categories of interest to human beings.

Experience has taught me that the above five categories are most likely to be immediately relevant to my seminar participants, and I assume that they may interest you as well. If they don't, you can substitute your own unique categories in each of the following exercises.

Let's first examine what seems to be the foundation for the four other major forms of wealth: emotional wealth.

The Big One: Emotional Wealth

Emotional wealth is the same as emotional well-being. If you can manage emotional resources, you can manage resources in virtually any other category.

This wealth, I believe, is the real secret of the truly wealthy. Intelligent management of emotions supports and makes wealth in the other four major areas possible, so we're going to look at emotions in some detail.

First, let's deal with a major misconception. Emotional wealth does not mean that you live in a world without problems, or that you constantly experience total bliss. Emotional wealth is an ability to live with great abundance and balance, because of a conscious effort to cultivate positive emotions and move away from negative ones.

People who live in a state of emotional wealth consistently find ways to allow their positive emotions to guide them to a state of overall well-being—and insure wealth in other areas of their lives.

To achieve emotional wealth you must develop strategies for staying in touch with your emotions and promote a constructive response to new emotional patterns.

To develop emotional wealth, you must be willing and able to maintain full emotional awareness.

That point is worth emphasizing! If you don't acknowledge the emotions you're feeling, you can't respond to them effectively. One way to do this is to analyze negative emotions and "mine" them for positive purposes, in the same way miners sift through a modest-looking deposit, but sometimes find gold. Our emotions can change from negative to positive in the blink of an eye. You have doubts? Well, you're certainly not alone. When I reach this point in my seminars, there is usually someone sitting in the audience who feels compelled to stand up and say, "You say I can change my emotions that easily? Okay, Tony, how do I shift my emotions around so that I won't feel lousy about getting up and going to work tomorrow morning?"

That is a fair question with a clear answer. Here's a great way to shift your emotions—and to claim your emotional wealth—starting when you want! Tomorrow morning, don't focus on the activity you hate—in this case, dragging yourself out of bed to get ready for work. Instead, focus on the *reason* you don't want to get up. Let's say it's your boss, a person with whom you don't have a particularly great relationship. Your job now is to ask yourself some key questions about the cause of the negative emotion.

§ What can I do today that is positive, appropriate, and encouraging that would show my boss an entirely different side of myself and my abilities?

§ What can I do today that is positive and appropriate that would help me see a different and better side of my boss?

If you focus in on questions like these with full attention, an open mind, and a nonjudgmental attitude, I think you'll find that these questions will leave you feeling energized and downright brilliant! By the time you get out of the shower, you will have unearthed five or six intriguing, energizing strategies for improving the area that had you feeling grumpy a few minutes before.

Another (equally important) way to maintain emotional awareness is to acknowledge one or more positive emotions for later use. You may remember how I did this when I needed a positive result in an otherwise disappointing business situation: I recalled my gift and the positive emotions associated with it, and much to my surprise, I got the desired outcome.

Use the techniques we've discussed earlier in this book to "program" your positive emotions, so you can summon them on command and at a moment's notice.

~

If we want to be wealthy in every aspect of our lives, we must learn to interrupt our negative emotions, and control and harness the power of our positive emotions—so we can put them to good use.

~

You, and only you, have direct control over internal emotions. Even so, you will experience an emotional state that you find both unproductive and extremely difficult to dislodge. Usually, this will come about for one of two reasons:

§ because you are interacting with a person whom you respect deeply, or who has immense importance in your life, or

§ because the situation you face represents a prominent element of some goal you associate with happiness in the present or the future.

In both instances, the strategies I've just outlined may not always see you through as quickly as you'd like. This is because of deep (and perhaps long-established) associations with the person or goal in question. Or, the way you've chosen to represent the situation to yourself may be inherently unproductive. You may well have set yourself up in a "game"—one that you are likely to lose.

In these instances, you must be prepared to change the "rules of the game" to make a positive outcome more likely.

Let's say you've got a rejection problem—you're finding it hard to grow in a certain area, because you feel, at a very deep level, that the next time you take action, you're likely to be rejected. What have you got to back up that belief? Plenty of past experience! Every time you've tried to do X, and things didn't pan out, you've felt rejected!

In such a situation, you must—repeat, must—look more closely at the rules of the game you've established for yourself. Here's my rule on that score; I bet it will work for you, too.

~

You're never rejected until you give someone or something permission and power to reject you!

~

Mentoring over one million professionals has proven to me that rejection is a big issue for many people. So, I want to tell a story that will illustrate how changing the rules can yield significant emotional benefits.

Picture a skittish 15-year-old (me), taking in his umpteenth Catholic Youth Organization dance, thinking, "Tonight's the night!" I was so eager to dance my first dance that I was trembling. I was ready to jump at any chance to dance with one of the pretty girls standing across the room. (This was back in the days when boys and girls were carefully segregated at such events!)

My best friend Richie knew what was going through my mind, and he knew I had my eye on a particular young lady. "Go ahead, ask her," he whispered. "All she can do is shoot ya down!" Well, Richie's advice made a certain amount of sense. Even then, I was willing to take a risk to develop a future relationship, which is certainly a good outlook! As it happens, though, it's not the *only* relevant advice on the topic of building a relationship. But I'm getting ahead of my story.

I walked across that wide hall and asked the young lady whether she'd like to dance.

She said no.

The return trip to the boys' side was a mortifying experience, one I wouldn't wish on any adolescent. But I vowed not to take "no" for an answer. Unfortunately, I didn't think to examine my tactics that night! I kept asking the *same* question over and over again: "Do you want to dance?"

All told, I heard a "no" response to that question six times that evening! That made 12 trips across that long dance floor— a total my buddy Richie was sure to remind me of on the walk back home.

By the time the next Friday came around, I was seriously considering going shopping with my mother at the A&P, rather than take part in another "walk-a-thon" at the CYO hall! Who needed the rejection? Fortunately, I had a talk with my older brother Al that afternoon. Al had more experience in these sorts of things, and he passed along some advice I'll never forget. It was a suggestion that changed not only my immediate social prospects, but also my entire life!

Al told me that when a girl gave me a "no" answer, it wasn't *me* being rejected—it was the dance!

Do you see what he did? He helped me to change the rules of my game! My old rules had said: "Girl says no—Tony has been rejected." Al straightened me out! He showed me that the new rule needed to be: "Girl says no—*the dance* has been rejected!"

What a concept! I truly believe that when Al talked about rejection, he laid the groundwork for my entire future, my professional career, and my personal life!

At that time, I was more interested in his immediate goal of improving my social life. Al gave me a couple of other pointers that followed up on the basic principle he'd outlined. That night, I put them to work at the dance—and every time the music played (except for the tunes I sat out to tease my buddy Richie a little bit) I was dancing!

What changed? Well, as I say, I followed Al's advice. That afternoon, he told me, "Bro, if you want to get the right answers, learn to ask the right questions!" Wiser words were never spoken! That night, every time I approached a potential dance partner, I'd ask her, "Do you know how to do the cha-cha?" The answer was usually, "Of course!" Then I'd ask, "How would you like to show everyone on the floor how good you are?" Without a word, the girl I was talking to would always take my hand and step onto the dance floor with me!

Asking the right questions—of others and of ourselves—is vitally important. When you feel a strong self-doubt emotion after someone or something has said "no" to you—it's absolutely essential that you acknowledge the emotion and find its source. Is it based on a situation you can change by "altering the rules" and asking different questions?

The fastest way to get in the habit of asking yourself the right questions to control your emotional state may be to change your vocabulary. Try using these alternative words when you need to modify your emotional outlook.

Limiting Word	Empowering Word
Lost	Looking
Scared	Thrilled
Stupid	Seeking
Failing	Learning
Overwhelmed	Absorbed
Sad	Reflecting
Worried	Curious
_____	_____
_____	_____
_____	_____

Jot down some of your own words and replacements on the last few lines.

Let me repeat that emotions are the most important category of wealth. Once you use tools like these to manage emotions, use your emotional resources to move closer to wealth, as *you* define it, in the other four major areas. If you don't manage emotions—if emotions are creating a storm that blows you to and fro like a ship without a rudder, without pattern or purpose—then none of what follows in this chapter will be of much use to you.

Put your emotions to work! Create a wealthy life!

What Wealth Means to You

Take a moment to define exactly what wealth means in your career, interpersonal relationships, in terms of personal development, and in your finances.

Take four blank sheets of paper. Label them as follows:

Career wealth

Interpersonal wealth

Personal wealth

Financial wealth

At the top of each sheet, write a heading for each separate category: "My definition of career wealth is… My definition of interpersonal wealth is," and so on.

Use a pencil because we'll make many changes.

Develop a 25-word statement that reflects your understanding of wealth in each category. Here's one of my statements:

Career Wealth:

I will continue to provide ways for our company and all of our employees to grow and realize the highest potential possible. I will strive to give them job security and improve our company by serving customers beyond their expectations. I will improve our fiscal well-being each year and provide greater benefits for employees and their families.

My picture will appear on the cover of an internationally known trade magazine. My peers will look upon me with respect and admiration. I will become more capable in all of the skills necessary to become one of the top ten speakers in the nation. I will improve my voice & delivery skills, listening skills, humor, body gestures, and stage presence. I will improve my ability to create intellectual work, and to express myself with words and stories. I will continue to find ways to share what I know with everyone having a sincere interest and desire to learn.

If you're tempted to fill in the blank with a negative answer—one that focuses on what you don't want, or on what you must stop doing to achieve a result in a certain area—start over! Thus, in the interpersonal area, the phrase "Stop fighting with my spouse" would need to be changed to something like "Improving communication with my spouse" or "Understanding my spouse's viewpoint on important issues."

Take as much time as you need to develop short first-draft statements in all four areas. Remember—use a pencil. You'll tinker with these entries!

Please stop now and develop your first-draft wealth statements for each category before you proceed any further in the book.

Welcome back! Take a close look at your entries now. Which positive words did you use to describe what wealth means to you in all four areas? Circle all the words and phrases that show up in more than one category. Consider including identical or similar positive words in all four definitions in your second draft.

Before rewriting, though, go back to the core values you identified in Chapter One—and assign appropriate values to the relevant wealth definitions. For instance, in the career wealth definition I shared a little earlier, appropriate and supporting core values would be:

- Trustworthy
- Honesty
- Forthright
- Loyal
- Esteemed

...and so on. In developing the second draft of your wealth definitions, think about ways to include these core values and *increase your own personal value* in a given area.

Do you remember the experience I related earlier in the book about being placed on probation for low sales performance? In order to win the customers I needed to keep my job, I had to find a way to show my core values and improve those values. By doing so, I automatically increased my own value—both to the customers and to my employer! I proved to myself that...

Increased personal value is directly related to career wealth, interpersonal wealth, personal wealth, and financial wealth!

Be sure you've incorporated some aspect of increasing personal value to each and every one of your wealth definitions. Most people highlight core values and identify areas for increased personal value during the second-draft phase. Identify areas where you can increase your personal value and emphasize core values in each of the four major wealth areas. Read through all the ideas that follow before you take time to develop the second draft of your wealth statements.

Increase Your Personal Value in...

Career Wealth:

 Enroll in a continuing education course to strengthen skills: That are required in your current position

That are not required in your current position but would increase your overall abilities and your value. (Example: Chelsea is the Director of Advertising for a food distributor. She decides to take a course on nutrition so she can better comply and communicate with the FDA in developing advertisements for a major food-processing corporation.)

That are required for the next highest level position in your company.

 Subscribe to and read typical trade journals in your industry.

 Join and participate in an association that supports your industry.

§ Volunteer, if possible, for any fund-raising activity that your company supports and that you believe in.

§ Make yourself available to mentor the next new member of your department.

§ Volunteer for focus groups, quality teams or other "for the good of the company" causes.

Interpersonal Wealth:

§ Invest more time and emotional energy in your interpersonal relationships.

§ Read supportive self-help material, articles, and books on the topics of becoming a better person and companion.

§ Read books on the topic of building listening skills and becoming a better conversationalist.

§ Try becoming unpredictable in a pleasant way. Use more of your creative ability to become spontaneous by initiating impromptu drives, movies, or walks.

§ Become a tourist in your own town. Take a weekend to discover or rediscover your town with someone special. Visit historical sites, local music haunts, or whatever else your town has to offer.

§ Swap chores for one week. Role-reversal is good exercise and it makes for stimulating conversation at parties!

§ Get in the habit of saying things like "Thank you," "I am sorry," "I love you," and "I appreciate your special talents and traits."

Personal Wealth:

§ Read at least twenty books each year: twelve self-help books and eight recreational books.

§ Attend seminars and workshops, when possible, that discuss topics you find interesting and that are necessary for personal growth.

§ Learn a new hobby! Basket weaving, pottery, windsurfing, roller-blading, sewing...

§ Give time to a worthy cause. Work one day a month at the local children's center or senior center.

§ Give a portion of your earnings to a needy family or charity.

§ Clean out your closet! Give away everything you haven't worn in the past six months.

§ Run an errand for someone needy or just as a courtesy. Next time you're going to the hardware store or supermarket, call your next door neighbor and ask if he or she needs anything.

§ Make it a habit to slow down and help someone cross the street; carry a package; open a door.

§ Smile! Say things like "Please" and "Thank you" more often.

§ Enjoy and experience nature first hand. Turn off the TV and take a hike!

Financial Wealth:

§ Subscribe to a periodical that discusses sound financial retirement plans or investment strategies.

§ If you invest in the stock market (and I suggest that you do) read the annual report of each company you invest money in.

§ Attend local seminars on financial independence. But beware of con artists or inexperienced "counselors." Check out everyone and everything before you take your checkbook out!

§ Find an advisor in your family, community, or company who can provide guidance and answer your questions free of charge.

§ Join an investment club. Here again, there may be many to choose from in your area. These clubs can be educational, fun, and financially rewarding.

Even More on Career Wealth

Core values to highlight here tend to center around the acquisition of new job-related skills and experiences. Certainly, adding to your professional "arsenal" of accumulated knowledge and intellect is one of the best ways to increase your value in this area.

It's important to understand that intellect is as important as knowledge. Knowledge is raw information; intellect is the application of that knowledge, the understanding of how a particular piece of knowledge is used to obtain a particular result. If you stop and think about it, you'll probably realize that you've worked with many knowledgeable coworkers who somehow couldn't apply all their mental power to accomplish a particular task. Intellect is goal-oriented! Try to find some way to incorporate growth in this all-important area into your definition of career wealth.

Christy just completed a self-paced course on the Internet that enhanced her ability to work with spreadsheets. She takes her new knowledge and spends five or six hours one weekend to modify her department's budget forecasting forms on her own initiative. Then she presents them to her supervisor for consideration. Not only does Christy's department find them useful—but the entire division ends up using them! Christy is a more valuable resource than she was, and she put her intellectual strength to practical use!

Even More on Interpersonal Wealth

Core values to emphasize here may reflect a loving nature, compassion, flexibility, and similar essentials for any ongoing relationship with a friend or loved one.

The best way to improve any interpersonal relationship is simply to *increase your value to the other person*. That means you can't take the person for granted! Certainly, there are risks involved—you'll want to be sure that the relationship is a healthy one in which neither participant is being manipulated or taken advantage of—but the basic principle holds. To increase your value as a spouse, for instance, you may need to learn to control your temper or listen more compassionately when your partner talks about the day's events. Doing so will go a long way toward demonstrating your commitment to the relationship—and maybe even encourage your partner to grow in a way that supports you, too!

In finalizing your definition of wealth as it relates to interpersonal relationships, find some way to incorporate growth in an area that will have a positive effect on one or more important relationships in your life. Base this on your core values that support mutuality and continuing shared experience.

Dee is a single parent. She holds a full-time job but still finds the time to make her presence known at all of Timothy's baseball, soccer, basketball, and school band performances. When I asked Dee how she finds the time, she simply says: "I tell myself, that when Tim has kids of his own, he won't recall what I did when I was at work—but he'll always remember that I was at all of his games! Then I'm motivated to find a way to make the schedule work."

Even More on Personal Wealth

Here, a core value is knowledge *for its own sake*. In other words, when it comes to personal growth, give yourself permission to celebrate core values that allow you to learn what you want to learn about, whether or not you can put it to immediate practical use.

Hobbies and avocations—things we do because we want to, not because we have to—increase our overall value because they give us a sense of balance. But there's a catch: You have to stretch yourself! You have to find areas where you can benefit from the words, ideas, or actions of others that are more advanced than you in a given discipline. Perhaps that discipline is playing squash; perhaps it's Shakespearean studies. Whatever it is, it should keep you alert and figure prominently in your second-draft definition of wealth in the area of personal growth.

Allison loves arts and crafts; she has centered her creations on floral designs made from dried and cut flowers and herbs.

For the holidays last year, Allison made each family member a lovely centerpiece. Allison's grandmother shared hers with the other seniors at the center she visits. The facility director asked Allison if she would like to show the folks at the center how to make arrangements—and soon she was teaching a course at six area rest homes. She brings children from a local foster home along to many of the classes—and enriches the days of both young and old. Allison does all of this without monetary reward, but the value it adds to her personal wealth is immeasurable. She's made important new friendships with at least half a dozen students who are "young at heart!"

Even More on Financial Wealth

Core values to consider are foresight, persistence, detail orientation, and follow-through—assets that help you carry out projects and establish workable plans.

Wealth in the financial area may ultimately be measured by dollars and cents—but it should first be measured by plans that bring those sums into existence! In this definition, you must get specific about the ways you make planning your financial future a "must have" priority, so you can learn how to use the discretionary income you have today to guarantee a secure future. Build this definition around exciting goals (that dream of sailing the South Pacific on a beautiful sailboat). Then be sure to include specifics to help turn that dream into reality (finding out exactly what is and isn't coming to you under the provisions of your 401K plan).

Retirement Alert!

The following four rules of retirement may prove useful for all of us over the age of fifteen:

§ Don't wait until you reach "retirement age" to experience aspects of your retirement dream. Do you want to sail? Do it during your next vacation. Do you want to travel around North America in a motorhome? Fly to Seattle and rent a

motorhome and drive to Anchorage. Do it now! You may
find the dream isn't right for you, so why not test-drive
that dream on a modest scale?

§ Don't—I repeat, don't—expect your employer to provide
100 percent of your retirement income.

§ Don't—I repeat, don't—expect the US government (or
any other government) to provide 100 percent of your
retirement income.

§ Return to the beginning of this list.

Take time now to rewrite all four of your wealth definitions,
incorporating your thoughts and ideas from the advice you've
just read. I suggest that you don't proceed until you've done this.

~

Congratulations! You're now in possession of the information
to create wealth on your own terms. You know what wealth
means to you in each of the four major areas.

Setting and Fine-tuning Goals

If you're like most people, the process of drafting and redrafting
your wealth definitions has left you feeling motivated to energize one or more goals in each of the wealth categories. (Often,
the process of revision leads to the formulation of goals you
realize you should have been focusing on before, but weren't.)
Let's take a moment to talk about goals, plans, and objectives in
each of the critical wealth areas of our lives.

There are five proven steps to goal setting and achievement.
You can use this five-step process to revamp existing goals, to
develop new goals, and to make virtually any goal a reality. Sound
exciting? It is!

1 Give birth to a priority.

2 Suspend self-limiting judgment.

3 Create a goal list.

4   Make one goal a priority.

5   Take action!

Here's the "lowdown" on each of the five steps.

Step One: Give Birth to a Priority

When we give something priority, we put it on the "front burner" of our minds, so we can watch it closely and monitor it with great diligence. At the same time, we tell our minds to do what amounts to a keyword search in our internal databases, and ask it to share all the relevant results with us as soon as possible!

I'm not exaggerating. When you create a priority, everything related to that particular subject is brought to the forefront of your mental processes. If you have relevant information "on file," your brain is going to track it down and make it available. This remarkable supporting response is made possible by your brain's reticular activating system. The simplest way to describe this system is to say that it effectively uses your brain's information networks.

This process sounds impressive, because it is! As awesome as the power of your brain is, though, you're probably more familiar with its handiwork than you realize.

For instance, have you made a major purchase recently—say, an automobile, big-screen TV, VCR, or new designer dress? If so, you may have found that, after your purchase, you began to notice lots of other cars that were the same model as yours, or other TVs or VCRs on sale for less then you paid, or someone else wearing "your" dress! (While you were still in "evaluative" mode, you may also have noticed that your attention was drawn to models and advertisements in a similar way.)

Your mind is at work! If you invested a great deal of time, effort, and energy in the process of making the best possible choice before committing your money, your mind accepted that priority, and began networking to retrieve relevant information. That you finalized the purchase was *not* as dramatic a priority, so your brain kept processing for a couple of weeks, just to be on the safe side!

Imagine what could happen if you took advantage of that same process to establish a priority in your mind that had to do with an important future goal. Your mind would begin to notice related goals and desires that had a direct bearing on the "front burner" goal, and it would automatically draw your attention to actions, ideas, and individuals that could help attain your objective.

Take a moment now and establish one driving, overwhelming priority in each of your wealth areas. Remember, a priority is anything you successfully move to the "front burner" of your mind— anything you choose to make absolutely impossible to ignore.

Don't make the mistake of identifying a "priority" that doesn't or can't command your full attention. Your brain will ignore it! Consider the example we just discussed. For most of us, purchasing an automobile is a big deal! Your brain recognizes how much importance you place on that purchase, and acts accordingly.

You must identify one similarly impossible-to-ignore priority for each wealth category now. Establish a big, energizing task or objective that will be impossible for your brain to ignore.

Here are some examples. Read them over, then identify four personal priorities and write them down on the appropriate sheets.

Career Priorities:

- Do everything possible to get a 20% raise and promotion by the end of next month.
- Before my next birthday, find another job that has no more than a 10-minute commute from the house.
- Approach my boss with a winning proposal so she'll let me telecommute three days a week, starting in October.
- Present a stellar solution to our production line bottleneck by the end of this year.

Interpersonal Priorities:

- ⚘ Starting this weekend, spend three hours each weekend on a joint hobby or activity with my companion.
- ⚘ Starting tonight, read to my son before he goes to sleep.
- ⚘ Starting now, look at my family members when they talk to me.
- ⚘ Starting tomorrow, with a smile on my face, help with domestic chores. Well, maybe starting next week!

Personal Priorities:

- ⚘ Starting this week, exercise every day for 20 minutes.
- ⚘ Starting tonight, eat a balanced diet and eliminate in-between meal snacks.
- ⚘ Learn three new ways to become a better listener by this time next month.
- ⚘ Learn to manage my stress level while at work and stop bringing my "work" home, starting today.
- ⚘ Financial Priorities:
- ⚘ Read my 401(K) information packet by next payday.
- ⚘ Subscribe to and read the local business paper starting with the next issue.
- ⚘ Talk to a certified financial planner by next April 15.
- ⚘ Balance my checkbook and consolidate my savings account by December 31st.

You'll notice that I've included a time frame with each of these priorities. Make sure that your list of priorities has an "estimated" completion time.

Step Two: Suspend Self-limiting Judgment

The big point here is not to allow prejudices or assumptions arising from past experience to distract you from a positive focus on that big new priority.

Past prejudices or assumptions have a fascinating effect on people. If you allow any self-limiting belief to influence your priorities, your future will be automatically lowered to past or present expectations. ("I'd love to win the big Wooly-Bully contest—but everyone in my family has always said that I wilt under pressure. Why should it be any different this time?")

In order to make it past the whirling undertow of self-limiting thinking, constantly remind yourself that the attainment of your goals is dependent on current situations and resources—not past obstacles or assumptions. Posing appropriate, energizing questions about your priorities is a great way to do this.

- If money were no object, what would I want my career to be?
- What can I do to find (or be) the most ideal life mate?
- What could I experience in my field of interest that I have avoided experiencing before, due to uncertainty or fear?
- How much money will I need to live on when I retire?

It is vitally important to remove each and every self-limiting judgment you connect with the most important aspects of wealth in your life! Set aside a little time for questions like the ones I have just outlined each and every day.

Step Three: Create a Goals List

I strongly suggest that you complete this step in at least one major area for each of the wealth categories. Start with the "front-burner" priority you committed to paper. Then take at least five minutes to do nothing but write down goals that arise from that energizing, impossible-to-ignore priority. Use as many additional sheets of paper as you need.

Set your alarm and write non-stop until the time expires. Don't worry about plausibility or about details associated with the goals you commit to paper. Don't even think about whether or not the goal is mature! Just write in broad terms, taking the widest possible perspective, for at least five minutes in each wealth category. That's 20 minutes total.

The only rule in this exercise is that your goal must directly relate to the priority you established earlier!

Let's take the Interpersonal Priority of "reading to my child every night before she goes to bed." Here's what a goals list might look like:

- Call the biggest, best day care center and find out if a book club exists for children's books. If so, join it immediately.

- Go to the biggest bookstore in town and to the library to preview books written for children Marisa's age; buy or borrow the three best books.

- Look into a book or course to introduce a second language to toddlers.

- Look into the benefits of accelerated learning methods.

- Look into where I might donate used children's books so we can share our gift with less fortunate children.

- Stop by the bookstore at our place of worship and check out what they have.

- Talk to David and see if he has any good suggestions. His daughter Jillian is Marisa's age.

Step Four: Make One Goal a Priority in Each Wealth Area—and Develop a Battle Plan

This step may take time, but is worth the effort. Please do not continue in the book until you have completed the process outlined below!

First, review your entire list of goals, and select one in each wealth category that is both important and energizing to you. (In the "reading to Marisa" example above, it might be the second item, visiting the local library and bookstore.) Circle that goal on your sheet, or highlight it with a colored marker.

Next, identify any conflicts between your goals and core value beliefs, qualities, and traits. Revise or replace goals—or identify which values, beliefs, qualities, and traits you need to enhance or change altogether. If one of my goals is to retire at age 55 with a $75,000 annual income stream, and to have my house and car paid off, that's great! But if I'm currently 35 years old, and one of my core traits is ultraconservatism in financial matters, I have a conflict on my hands! I may have to learn how to be more of a risk-taker, and more of an opportunity-seeker to attain my financial goal.

Next, identify and fulfill any subsidiary goals before you take action on your main goal. Take the time to determine whether your most important goal is dependent on any other goal. In some cases, your number one goal will stand alone—it won't require you to complete anything else beforehand. That's fine. For most highly energizing goals—having a short story printed in the *New Yorker*, say—there are other goals that must be taken into account first. You will want to find out whether the magazine requires an agent to make submissions, and whether to format your submission in a particular style. You will also want to learn what short stories previously published in the magazine have in common. All of these factors will have an effect on your battle plan, the way you put your steps in order. When you're ready, focus on them constantly!

Step Five: Take Action

There is no doubt in my mind that if you have taken the time and mental energy to complete the exercises in this chapter you will now be ready to take action. I can think of only one thing to ask that will motivate you to do so.

  §   Who (not what) do you love the most on planet earth?

Is it a son, daughter, spouse, parent, companion, friend, or pet iguana? I strongly suggest that you share the work that you've done in this chapter with that person (or iguana). Share it right now. Show the person what your wealth lists look like, what your priorities are, and how the battle plan arising from your goal list is shaping up. Explain what you plan to accomplish in each major area of your life.

Oh, and One More Thing...

Have you completed all the work in this chapter? (I know there's a lot. If you answered "yes," take your left hand and put it on your right shoulder. Give yourself a pat on the back. You've done an outstanding job!

Waiting in the Wings

Each and every time I get ready to take the platform and deliver a speech, and I hear the announcer introducing me, I realize the importance of being the very best I can be in that moment. Understand: I'm not striving for perfection in each and every aspect of my life, or holding myself to an impossible standard. I'm giving the task at hand my all. As I listen to what the announcer is saying, I get excited about the prospect of listening to Tony Parinello!

Why wait for an "event" to share your unique gifts with others? Why wait for a special occasion to get others (or yourself!) excited about what you have to offer? Why not make every day a special one—a day when you take the excitement you feel while waiting in the wings and move it center stage?

Your road to success starts here and now. Today, right now, I want you to start treating every moment as though you were waiting offstage—and you've just heard the announcer say your name!

I'm not talking about becoming an egomaniac, of course. I'm talking about finding ways to tell yourself first, and then everyone else with whom you come in contact, that you're a special person. Regardless of what's happened in the past, regardless of what may happen in the future, you are alive in this moment, and you have something unique to offer!

Life is a mass of transitions. Don't deny them or cower in fear before them. Celebrate them! There is no beginning, no entrance you can make on the stage of life that is not an exit from somewhere else. There is no departure, no setback in this life that does not point you toward a new opportunity.

"Ladies and gentlemen, it gives me great pleasure to introduce you to…"

It looks like you're up. Break a leg!

~ *Chapter 10* ~

Wisdom

The final chapter of a book can be tricky, for both author and reader. For my part, I want to celebrate this final section by reaching some conclusions and offering several new insights to assist you in putting what you've learned to work in the following weeks, months, and years. (The alternative is simply to bid you good luck as you travel through the world, but I don't really think you need luck. If you did, I wouldn't feel as if I'd served you the best way I could.)

I've read my fair share of self-improvement books, and I've learned that any personal development book is only as valuable as the ideas one is motivated to implement *after* the final chapter. Haven't we all been let down in this area before? We see an idea, learn a new angle, get excited about it, and think, "I'll have to find a way to put that into practice... tomorrow." Then tomorrow never comes! I want this book to make the difference for you in the long term, and I want to start right now.

Here's your secret weapon: wisdom.

My own experience is that the best resource for putting ideas into long-term action is wisdom. Wisdom takes advantage of everything you already possess and keeps you from believing you have access to tools you haven't yet acquired. Wisdom is one of the most critical qualities and traits when it comes to harnessing the Power of Will for long-term benefits in your life. Developing wisdom is what we'll focus on here, in the final chapter.

What I Mean When I Talk about Wisdom

I think we all have an intuitive sense of what the word "wisdom" means, but let's nail down a definition before we proceed.

~

When you have common sense, you know right from wrong. When you possess wisdom, you do what's right!

~

Put another way: Wisdom means turning the stuff you know into a sound course of action, or a sound course of inaction, by circumstance. (Often, choosing not to respond at all is the best possible course of action.) Wisdom basically means giving yourself the best advice—the advice you would give to a loved one facing a similar challenge—and then following that advice yourself.

Some people mistake wisdom for knowledge. As important as knowledge is, it should not be confused with the ability to take what you have learned and put it to practical use in any situation. Often, wisdom—not mere technical knowledge or book learning—is essential to resolve or mediate two potentially opposing points of view. Those points of view exist within one person (when there is an internal struggle) or among two or more people. Ignoring the number of people involved, the problem of having to decide between opposing viewpoints is common and occasionally difficult to resolve.

How to Recognize the Wise

People who are merely knowledgeable tend to panic when called upon to reconcile opposing viewpoints. Wise people usually are *more relaxed* when they must find a way to "fit a square peg into a round hole." They know exactly what their experience base is (and isn't); they know exactly when to rely on their own abilities and insights (and when to reach out to others). They're worth observing closely. If you have a choice between picking a person who is a knowledgeable mentor in a certain area, or picking a wise person, I strongly suggest that you pick the "wise" gal or guy every time!

Here are six more ways to recognize truly wise people.

1 *They pick their causes carefully.* They know that sometimes even the most valiant fight may not be worth the potential loss it entails. Under other circumstances, adopting a "hopeless cause" is an important way to broadcast and reinforce key values and set a best practices example. Wise people realize it is up to them—not outside forces—to assign value to the campaigns they take on (or decline). Think for a moment. How many causes have you taken on in the past year that you shouldn't have, where you knew it was a mistake to make a commitment from the start? In the future, ask yourself these questions *before* taking the jump: Can I actually improve this situation? Have I improved similar situations? What will happen if my involvement makes this situation worse?

2 *They finish what they start.* Stop and think about it. Don't people you truly respect have a habit of completing the critical goal, dream, desire, or tasks they took on? I have never met a person I considered truly wise in a given area who was incapable of completing key projects. However, I have met many people whose personal lives (and careers) seemed forever unfinished. On big and small issues, they couldn't seem to reach the "finish line" no matter what they did. Perhaps they can't see the forest through the trees. Maybe they don't know the consequence of living with incomplete goals, dreams, and desires. Finishing what you start—and not taking on what you can't finish—is a particularly important trait of wisdom, and one worth reinforcing at every possible opportunity. If you are sitting in your office or home as you read this paragraph, survey your surroundings and ask yourself: "How many projects or commitments have I started but left unfinished? What evidence of those projects or commitments can I see here? How has the inability to follow through in these areas affected the image I projected to individuals depending on me? What effect did this habit have on my relationships? Have I been the best possible role model?"

3 *They have impeccable timing.* They don't just endure the seasons (although they certainly know how to think in the long term); they *utilize* the seasons. They know what to plant, how and when to plant it, how and when to water it, how and when to fertilize, how and when to harvest—and they act appropriately on that accumulated knowledge. Think of a current challenge you face in your personal, business, or financial life. Are all of your actions in accordance with the seasons? Are you patiently waiting for a result or pushing too hard? Are you expecting too much from someone or something? Are your expectations set too high, given what you know of the possible outcomes? Have you left yourself open for a repeated disappointment?

4 *They don't take shortcuts.* They have certain values that they simply refuse to compromise. They are not habitually stubborn, but they know when it makes sense to draw a line. Ill-advised departures from one's guiding principles can carry huge costs: lower self-worth, lower esteem, damaged reputation, and damaged self-image, to name just a few. Wise people know that the short-term benefit to cutting corners in their core value areas are usually far outweighed by the long-term price. Think of someone you know that takes the easy way out, the shortcut. Do you look to that person for advice or wisdom? Or do you look to someone who stays the course and goes the distance? For the next 30 days make a conscious effort to eliminate value-compromising shortcuts from your personal, business, financial, and recreational endeavors. Then evaluate your results!

5 *They're willing (and eager) to philosophize.* I don't mean that they spend all of their time in idle speculation. Wise people know how to distance themselves and get the proper perspective on a problem. They don't push too hard. They're skilled at the art of taking a mental "time out" when it's to their advantage. When faced with a big decision, they generally view every possible angle. They play with the situation a little bit before committing one way or another. Then they settle on a possible course of action, and before embracing it, ask themselves: Will I, at any point in time, have any regrets from my action or decision in this area? If so, how serious are those regrets in the grand scheme of things?

It's interesting to note here that the word "philosophy" comes from the Greek word "philosophos" which means, "to love wisdom." How can you learn to love wisdom? Perhaps by using the exercises in every chapter in this book to develop a better understanding of whom you are and where you're going. The true philosopher uses rational considerations to maintain a serene, temperate, and controlled resigned attitude. At the next opportunity, ask yourself, "Why am I living the life I am currently living?" Take a half-hour or so to explore all the possible answers!

6 *They turn envy into energy.* Wise people are happy with what they have and who they are. That doesn't mean that they don't want to grow and prosper. They know the importance of being happy with what is taking place in the here and the now. They don't become disconsolate over another person's "good luck" or their own seeming "bad luck." If they do become inspired to change something in their lives, instead of envy, they put the necessary energy forth to accomplish or acquire what they've envisioned. Think for a moment. Do you envy anyone? If so, why? Can you afford the energy that habit requires? Note the difference between energy and admiration! Envy saps energy and poisons relationships; admiration of another's positive traits is a supreme compliment that helps you focus on what you need to improve in your life.

If you've taken the time to review the six characteristics just discussed and asked the appropriate questions, you should have a good grip on your current level of wisdom. The challenge now is to deepen your wisdom, and to do a better job of showing others the best practices associated with this gift!

Stepping Stones to Wisdom

One great way to increase your wisdom is to spend years in the company of wise people who will share their insights. That should probably be a strategy unto itself, but the truth is, it's a rather difficult, long-term job! What else can we do?

I believe there are more immediate steps to bring wisdom to areas that make the most difference in our lives. I also believe that we should take those steps sooner, rather than later!

Yes. We can begin the journey toward wisdom right here and right now! And since wisdom, like success, is a journey, and not a destination, we can all be wiser today than we were yesterday. Once we start the cycle of wisdom in earnest, we'll notice that it has a way of perpetuating itself. Fortunately, it's relatively easy to get hooked on wisdom; but like many other life-affirming traits, wisdom still requires that we take the first step. The "wisdom system" has been set up in such a way that every step of the journey counts, and it may well be that the early steps count most of all.

We shouldn't wait for our AARP card, or until we learn everything the people we respect most have to teach, to begin the all-important process of expanding, using, and showing our wisdom. Once we begin that process, we will learn how to use the tools at our disposal. That includes all the ideas you've studied in this book! Once we begin that process, we will know where we are, who we are, and what we face. We won't try to delude ourselves or anyone else.

~

The wise person knows that the truth will still exist,
even if he or she should attempt to ignore it.

~

In order to enhance our own wisdom on a daily basis, and support it over time, we must do the following:

- § Celebrate the debate.
- § Empower others.
- § Show compassion.
- § Provide constructive critiques in appropriate situations.
- § Use experience consciously, not automatically.

Let's look at these five essential steps to make wisdom a daily reality.

Step One: Celebrate the Debate

We may think of the word "debate" as describing an intense, bitter, possibly unrewarding personal exchange. Wise people likely view the debate process (internal or external) as the *constructive* merit evaluation of a particular statement or course of action. For the wise person, "debate" is less of a reason to raise one's blood pressure and more an intuitive process likely to illuminate what he or she knew, at some level, to be right all along. Wise people use the debating process as an aid to intuition, and to track down additional information worth considering.

Wise people don't shun debates or turn them into personal grudge-settling sessions. They follow them with a sense of curiosity and adventure until the right approach appears, seemingly of its own volition.

Such a technique is both a valid method for evaluation of one's personal priorities and tactics, and an effective personal management tool. Wise people know how to open and continue debates that don't degenerate into (internal or external) ego-driven conflicts, but illuminate the other side's best motives.

You'll find that individuals with wisdom:

- § Listen to all sides of an issue.
- § Avoid jumping to conclusions.
- § Don't pass judgment on anyone or anything in the process.

§ Never act before essential facts are understood and out on the table.

§ Focus on events, ideas, and situations—not people—when offering advice.

Wise people know that debating is more effective than attempting to dictate particular courses of action. The first process allows all the participants "ownership" of the final conclusion and uses more than one mind, viewpoint, and opinion to develop that conclusion. Issuing orders, on the other hand, can have only one of two effects:

1 The person shuts down and does exactly what the dictator orders, which eliminates the possibility of any additional creative thought.

2 The person begins thinking about ways (obvious or subtle) to rebel against the dictator—or sabotage the result—in an attempt to prove a point.

Wise people are constantly initiating open-minded, open-ended debates with themselves and others because they know that, in situations that make the most difference, *people only act on their existing inclinations*—not on outside values or priorities. Debates clarify what's positive, what's constructive, what's workable, and what's most creative, among those existing inclinations.

～

Dictators think they compel creative action.
In fact, they only terrify, and they generally
can't even do that for very long.

～

Think of a time when someone asked you for advice—you gave it—and the other person actually ended up following it. During the exchange, did you hear the other person say things like?

§ Yeah, I know. I should do that.

You're absolutely right. I've been telling myself that for a month.

 I've felt that way all along—I just needed to hear someone else say it.

Rarely, if ever, will someone take our advice to do something that he or she didn't already have some inclination to do. It's the job of the wise person to use debating (rather than dictating) to bring the most creative, constructive initiatives to the surface—not to worry who will eventually receive credit for a good idea.

Practice nonjudgmental exploration of all the options with yourself and others. When a good idea arises during a debate, and another person embraces it, don't attempt to take credit. Let the other person feel it was his or her idea all along. Because when you get right down to it, at the deepest level, it was!

"How did that book report you were working on turn out?"

"What a trauma! I thought it was great work, but I almost lost a whole grade on that thing, Dad."

"Really? What happened?"

"It took me two whole hours to find the report! I was up late Sunday night going through my room. If I'd handed it in a day late, I would have dropped a whole letter."

"Wow! How long did it take you to write it, anyway?"

"An hour and a half. What a waste of time that was, scouring my room!"

"Think so?"

"Yeah. You know, I think I'm going to try to sneak up on my desk and get it organized tonight, so I don't have to go through that again."

(Question: What happens to the above dialogue if the father responds with "I told you so," instead of "How long did it take you to write it, anyway?")

Step Two: Empower Others

Ready for another secret? Wisdom really *is* a matter of keeping score. The more people you affect positively by empowering them, the more points go up on your scoreboard! This is probably the best game ever created—because your opponent is you!

As I've already mentioned, having wisdom is *not* a matter of trying to control, manipulate, or dominate others! In most cases, power means struggle—testing one's strength against another, and attempting to scratch out a "win" at the expense of someone else. This is not the power wise people seek. Instead, they search for a path allowing everyone to achieve. They look for ways to get major emotional and spiritual payoffs by *adding*, not diminishing, power and influence to the lives of the people they contact. How do they do it?

❀ *They help others move toward "expert" status.* Everyone is somebody else's expert in some area. What really matters is that the expertise is shared! Here's a perfect example: I'm a weekend warrior with a surfboard—even after a year and a half, I consider myself a novice surfer. That doesn't stop me from sharing the basics with people who are just beginning. The other weekend, Nick, a young boy I helped learn to stand up on his board, referred to me as "that surfer who really knows his stuff" while talking to his mother. I'd never thought of myself as good enough to be called a "surfer," much less a good one! On my way home, I realized that lesson had strengthened my own grasp of some essentials. Your own knowledge, talents, and interests are gifts best enjoyed when shared with others!

～

When you share expertise, you empower that person to become better—and you get better, too!

～

Look for ways to share what you know. Bear in mind that someone else is usually observing us, taking in our words, the gestures we use, and the attitudes we adopt. The number of people we influence over the course of a single day is truly amazing! Every person you sit next to, pass in traffic, or share an elevator with can be influenced by you, either positively or negatively. And, as a general rule, the younger that person is, the more likely he or she is to be influenced. Watch what you tell small children—overtly or otherwise—about the world and how it works.

❀ *They offer "best practices" examples.* It's not enough to know how to do something well! We must also know how to take action in a way that helps serve as the best practices example, and we must develop a level of optimism capable of making someone's day better. If you doubt this important ability, consider your own life. Think of the last time you were in a bad mood, facing down the whirlwind of obstacles and setbacks, and getting down on yourself. How grateful were you when you finally came across something that turned your head around? It may have been a child who brightened your day, or a bumper sticker that made you laugh, or a colleague that served as your best practices example in maintaining control over emotional states! Did who or what you encountered make you grateful?

❀ *They give heartfelt compliments.* If you're looking for a simple, fast, and effective way to empower someone and put an instant boost into that person's day, offer a well-founded and sincere compliment. The last time someone did this for you, didn't you suddenly feel like you could take on the world—or at least make headway on the day? We all like recognition (particularly public recognition). Compliments cost nothing to give—and they offer a tremendous potential return on investment. If you keep the compliments valid, appropriate, and realistic, they'll make both you and the other person feel great and lay the groundwork for a lasting positive relationship.

Practice building up your compliment-giving muscle. Are you going out to breakfast, lunch, or dinner today? If you do, and if you receive service worthy of sincere thanks, thank the server sincerely! Then, before you pay your bill, ask for the manager. Tell the manager exactly what you thought of the meal! You might even take the time to write a thank-you note to the chef. If you've never done this, you're in for a treat. It's a delightful experience, and it's a great way to establish yourself as a "regular" at a restaurant. (You get even better service and food the next time around!)

Step Three: Show Compassion

~

People who have wisdom must have a passion for being compassionate.

~

What do I mean by that? I mean that wise people learn to become highly motivated to offer help in a certain area in a *way* that's likely to help other people. To grow in this aspect of wisdom, we must constantly reinforce our instincts to reach out and make another person's life better in a tangible way—until we have built up an intense, powerful enthusiasm for helping. The best way to do this may be to find opportunities to volunteer at your local church, community or service group—but these certainly aren't the only ways!

At every opportunity, we must remind ourselves how to love the act of helping. We shouldn't make it a requirement that we like (or even know) the person receiving help. All we must do is get into the habit of giving in a way that makes a positive difference.

When I was a boy growing up in Hoboken, New Jersey, we had an upstairs neighbor named Anna-Marie who became a friend of my mother's. For a long time, Anna-Marie and her husband were having difficulty making ends meet. My mother would send me upstairs on Friday evenings with a pot full of "leftovers" for Anna-Marie. After a while, I realized that my mother must have been cooking these "leftovers" intentionally for her, knowing full well that she would be able to use the food to feed her in-laws (who came to visit every Saturday). Anna-Marie, too, must have known that the pounds of pasta, the endless trays of ziti and linguine, couldn't really have been "leftovers"—unless my family had been issuing dinner invitations to the New York Yankees every Friday night!

Anna-Marie's hard times eventually eased up. She and my mother were very close over the years, and I think only part of that had to do with the food. The friendship was based on the love that guided the way that food had been offered. This was an instance where my mother knew that offering help in a way that another person could accept was a central element of compassion.

My mother was the great teacher in my life regarding compassion. Her actions spoke far more eloquently then her words, but her words were pretty darned good, too. She always told me:

§ "You can't just hope for people, you have to help them."

Whom have you helped to improve lately? What strategies have you used to ensure that the help you offered was easy to accept? When the opportunity presents itself (it always does) act on it. Follow my mother's example—help the Anna-Maries in your world—send a batch of leftover ziti upstairs, whether it's left over or not! Just be sure you make it easy for the other person to accept your help.

Step Four: Provide Constructive Critiques in Appropriate Situations

This is a biggie!

Wise people know something that the rest of us often forget: people prefer critiques to criticism. Truly wise individuals rarely, if ever, criticize anyone or anything. They learn, through constant practice, to offer critiques focused on helping expand something positive—not to simply identify what does not work. You may remember the classic *Peanuts* comic strip in which Lucy compiled a detailed fault list of all her friends, and passed them around for everyone's benefit. For some strange reason, this didn't go over well.

Wise people content themselves to be available to provide critiques that avoid the following common pitfalls:

- § Any form of the phrase, "I told you so." (This instantly kills any meaningful communication.)

- § Any attempt to manipulate, distort, or otherwise "stack" the facts of the situation the other person faces. (Efforts to dictate the other person's experience, reactions, or future options are always doomed to failure.)

- § Any hurried, negatively focused opinion. (Harsh and tactless conclusions about the problems and concerns of others— especially when delivered in haste—can make the other person feel more like a defensive basketball player than a valued friend, companion, team member, or relative.)

Wise individuals have the patience, understanding, and concern necessary to step back from a situation. They generally wait until others seek their advice to offer opinions. They do not allow personal grudges or past problems to determine the structure of a critique or the future.

How can you ensure that the help you pass along is more like a critique and less like criticism? There are two things to keep in mind here.

Check Your Ego at the Door

First, make it clear that your concern is not ego-driven. As a practical matter, this means you will place all the attention, interest, and energy you possibly can on the other person's concerns, and as little as you can on your own. Let's say a younger relative—perhaps your daughter—wants to discuss her plan to join the Peace Corps, rather than go to college. The *way* you react to the appeal will immediately tell the other person whose interests are driving the discussion and the pending decision.

One of the best ways to ensure that your ego isn't in the driver's seat is to focus on neutral questions. Consider these two possible responses to the Peace Corps announcement.

⚖ "The Peace Corps? What are you, crazy? After the grades you got in high school? After being named class valedictorian? Don't you realize what you'd be throwing away? Don't you realize what the rest of the family would say? You would be the first of any of Grandma and Grandpa Importanta's grandchildren not to go to college! I think that would give them both heart attacks! After all, you're the one we all assumed would go to Harvard. Now you're thinking of going off to Indonesia and build huts? You'll make your mother and me sick with worry. No, I really don't think the Peace Corps is for you, honey."

⚖ "The Peace Corps? Well, it's not what your mother and I expected, that's for sure. What is it that excites you about that kind of work? [Listen to the answer you get.] What do you think the biggest challenges working overseas would be? [Listen to the answer you get.] Can you think of any possible drawbacks? [Listen to the answer you get.] Have you spoken to anyone who has worked in Indonesia on this kind of project? [Once again, listen to the answer you get.]"

The first response, which emphasizes only *our* concerns and fears, is more or less guaranteed to land you in the middle of a big, fat fight—or convince the other person that talking to you is pointless. The second response is far more likely to highlight areas of concern to both sides and lead to a realistic assessment of the pros and cons of such a major decision.

See the Person as an Individual—Not an Extension of Yourself

This has to do with what I call self-reflection—the tendency to want special individuals in our lives to follow our own agenda, or to do better than we did in a certain area. The problem of self-reflection is similar to ego-driven problems, but more complex. Self-reflection involves putting our values into the lives of other people and expecting them to behave as we would behave in a certain situation.

The most dangerous thing about self-reflection is that we may actually mistake it for altruism. After all, we're acting in the other person's best interests, aren't we? All we want is what's good for that person, and we may even put our own interests aside in order to help bring about "what's good" for him or her. The problem is that the person we're helping may not want or need the help because his or her goals and other factors may be different! Here, we're not concerned about our own shame, embarrassment, fear, or lack of social status. We may even endure great hardships to bring about what seems to be a positive outcome for the other person. What we've forgotten is that the critique we offer can only be helpful and uplifting if it assists the other person in doing what's right for him or her!

Let's say you waited until you were in your early thirties to get married—and your 22-year-old son asks for advice on whether he should marry his high-school sweetheart. It may be difficult to separate your priorities from the question, "What's right for my son in this situation?" You must avoid viewing the critique as an opportunity to deliver a lecture about what you would do in a similar situation, or what you have successfully done in the past. Put aside what you have done (or haven't done) or what you want (or don't want) for the other person. Focus on questions that help the other person identify potential obstacles and clarify underlying motives.

After you ask questions to make sure you understand the other person's motives, and you're ready to make your statement, do so using a "third-person" structure. At all costs, avoid statements like: "If I were you, I'd…" or, "Now, what you need to do is…" or, "When I was your age I…" or, "If you knew what was good for you, you'd…" or any other self-serving statements. Instead, stick to "detached" statements like:

- ♭ Situations like this may mean…
- ♭ Sometimes when people react to A with B, they find that C.
- ♭ Often, it looks like X is the case, but Y and Z sneak up while no one is looking.

The more neutral you make your statements, the more receptive the other person is likely to be.

There's an old German proverb that's appropriate here:

~

We think all the bells echo our own thoughts.

~

We cannot dictate the future of other people! Nor can we automatically impart our own experience to people we love. We can only support them as they make their own appropriate choices. If we're lucky, we may be able to throw light on the major factors that a loved one will be facing during a certain course of action. But we can never make another person's choice!

The fastest way to learn how to get your ego out of the picture is to use the following exercise. The next time a family member, companion, subordinate at the office, or peer solicits your opinion or advice, swap places before you open your mouth and share your insights. That's right—physically switch positions. For example, if a subordinate at the office asks your advice, say, "Ruth, that's a great question. Before I take it on, though, I want to try something. Here, why don't you sit in my chair behind my desk and let me sit where you are—and I'll ask you that same question. Put yourself in my position and see what happens when you try to answer your question." Then let the other person take a stab at the problem *before* you weigh in with your own advice! Changing places physically helps you change places emotionally and intellectually, too.

Step Five: Use Experience Consciously, Not Automatically

The wise are never prisoners of their own experiences. They do not simply respond in unfamiliar (or even familiar) circumstances. They react consciously, using what works and setting aside what does not. They don't carry around any "baggage" that they don't need for a particular journey.

This may well be the most difficult step to wisdom. In order to fulfill it, we must continually strive to recognize our prejudices or unproductive instinctive responses. We must understand these biases and obstacles fully and work to reduce or eliminate the paralyzing effects they can and do have on our wisdom, our own success, and the success of others. This is an ongoing quest, and you will never hear a wise person boast that he or she has completed it.

To the degree that there is one, the "trick" to using experience consciously lies in learning to assume that we can always learn more about a given situation. That is exceptionally difficult, because human beings are inherently attracted to easy answers. But we must dedicate ourselves to eliminating bias or strong but unproductive instinctive reactions while dealing with others.

By the way, it's important to recognize that a bias in favor of a person, course of action, or object can be just as devastating as a bias *against* a person, course of action, or object. The last manager you hired was well-organized, and turned a previously unproductive programming department around in only 30 days. This person "cracked the whip," and suddenly people in the department could meet deadlines more readily, offer more creative ideas, and deliver on high-revenue projects with no problem. Could the same person be an effective manager for your struggling sales department? Maybe, maybe not. If your sales staff is stocked with former high achievers who are used to operating independently, they may perceive this person as an outsider who does not understand their world. They may become demoralized when the "crack the whip" campaign begins. The wise person will tabulate the similarities and differences in the two work settings, avoid a thoughtless unproven assumption ("This person can turn around any problem department"), and then make the best possible choice.

In the end, the best way to summarize this final step is simply to say that the wise understand that they must constantly augment and expand their wisdom. They accept that even the highest and most valuable principles can easily be misused, and that the most hopeful guiding assumptions can lead to disaster if applied to the wrong facts. Wise people know that their wisdom is limited, and they work to ensure that their experience does more good than harm in any new situation.

Be a Hero

The last piece of advice I have to offer is that you pass on to others what you have learned here. Transfer the torch. Keep the learning experiences alive in your life by sharing them to benefit others. That's the only way to harness the Power of Will in the long term: use it to make your life and others' lives better. Use it to make this world a better place.

In the summers of my youth, my family traveled to Washington, DC. It amazes me now how much we were able to pack into our 1949 two-door Chevy: mom, dad, grandma, my brother Al, my sister Phyllis, and me, and enough food to satisfy the Italian Army Third Brigade. We bounced along the highways and byways, ate eggplant sandwiches, played Monopoly, sang Jerry Vale songs, and built memories that I have cherished my entire adult life. Not long after we reached the capital, we found ourselves staring at a long line of glittering white monuments and statues. I asked my brother Al what these people had done to deserve such recognition. I expected him to tell me something about war, about bravery under fire, about patriotism. Those all would have been good answers. But they weren't the answers my big brother Al passed along.

He looked me in the eye mischievously and arched his eyebrows in a way that said, "You really want to know?" Then he smiled. After a few seconds, he answered my question: "They're heroes, bro. They're just like you. Wise guys, only older."

Al had a way of looking at me that made me feel like my whole life was ahead of me, like anything was possible. That's how he looked at me after he said this about heroes. In that moment, I could tell that my brother believed in me, no matter what, and that he wanted me to know that I could be a hero, too, capable of living any life I chose.

Because my family believed I could do anything I wanted to when I grew up, I always assumed I could. Today, my childhood is my past, and my guiding lights have moved on to whatever awaits us after this life. They guide me in a different way now, a way that tells me to help others in a special way.

I truly believe we can do anything we desire, too. My hope as we end our time together is that you use the ideas you've been reading about to build the life you're supposed to lead, and that, when the opportunity presents itself (which it will), you'll remind someone else that anything is possible.

It is!

A Special Offer

~

It's time to turn Thinking and Dreaming
into Action and Living!

~

Your mentor, Anthony Parinello

Your investment in this book entitles you to access to the author's tele-mentoring program.

Anthony Parinello, mentor and success coach to more than one million professionals, is ready to guide you on your journey to greater fulfillment and abundance in all aspects of your life. Because you invested in this book, you can take full advantage of his unique one-of-a-kind opportunity!

Each month, you'll be able to join Anthony's teleconferencing calls, ask the questions that mean the most to you, and get the advice and inspiration you need to turn thinking and dreaming into acting and living! What's more, you'll be able to listen to other individuals as they make progress toward their goals. There is no charge for this coaching for purchasers of *The Power of Will*; all you will pay is a standard teleconferencing long-distance telephone fee for the call.

Here's what people have to say about Anthony's coaching:

> *"Anthony is energetic, inspirational, and real!"*
>
> Pat Sharpe, NYC

> *"I always expect to take some valuable 'tidbit'… this time I needed a bucket to carry away the treasures."*
>
> Sharon Auerbach, Chicago

"Anthony is for real! Real experience, real ideas, and a real commitment to his students' success."

Vinnie Deschamps, San Jose, CA

Act now! Register for your mentoring as soon as you purchase this book! Send your sales receipt (or a copy of it) along with your name, address and telephone number to:

Parinello Incorporated
P.O. Box 875
Julian, California 92036
Attention: Ms. Catherine Jones

A registration card will be sent to you outlining the details of the program.